ENGLISH UPRISING

PRAISE FOR ENGLISH UPRISING

'*English Uprising* is an essential guide for what can happen when those in power pander to prejudices over immigration instead of tackling them. Dr Stocker engagingly and comprehensively shows how small acorns of English nationalism sprouted into the 2016 Brexit vote. This book shows that while those being demonised may have changed, the language used to attack them remains the same - and those in politics and the media have been all too ready to embrace the scapegoating instead of challenging it. A vital read for anyone who wants to understand why we're on the cusp of living in Nigel Farage's world.'

**Owen Bennett, author of *The Brexit Club: The Inside Story
of the Leave Campaign's Shock Victory***

'Paul Stocker's highly readable book skilfully explores the ways Brexit has created new opportunities for the British far right to develop its agenda, and adds much needed historical context for those who want to understand populism in Britain today.'

**Dr. Paul Jackson, senior lecturer in history,
University of Northampton**

'A good introduction to the history of racism and xenophobia in Britain, which provides important context to current political debates.' **Daniel Trilling, *New Humanist***

'Paul Stocker has written a timely, well researched and engaging book on Brexit and the far right in Britain. It provides an important historical perspective on racism and anti-immigrant xenophobia in the country.'

**Dr Aaron Winter, senior lecturer in criminology
and criminal justice, Univeristy of East London**

ENGLISH UPRISING: BREXIT AND THE MAINSTREAMING OF THE FAR RIGHT

PAUL STOCKER

MELVILLE HOUSE UK

LONDON

English Uprising
First published in Great Britain in 2017 by
Melville House UK
8 Blackstock Mews
Islington
London N4 2BT

mhpbooks.com   facebook.com/mhpbooks   @melvillehouse

A CIP catalogue record for this book is available from
the British Library

ISBN: 978-1-9115451-0-1

Design by Jamie Keenan
Typeset by Octavo Smith Publishing Services

1 3 5 7 9 10 8 6 4 2

CONTENTS

INTRODUCTION

For many, the Brexit vote came as a shock. Britain's choice on 23 June 2016 to leave the European Union appeared at first glance an unfathomable and irrational act of self-mutilation. However, when looking at the historical context of the vote, perhaps the only surprise should have been that it was so close. The background to Brexit, which will be explored in this book, was one in which anti-immigration politics and xenophobic sentiment had risen to the forefront of British political debate. Rather than a recent development, this process had been decades in the making. Britain's vote was overwhelmingly influenced by negative attitudes to immigration and its perceived problems that were forged during and after the Second World War. Taking the EU vote as a point of entry, a key task of this book is to demonstrate Britain's decades-long fraught relationship with immigration and ethnic change. It will ultimately seek to establish the historical background to Brexit and how Britain arrived at the decision it did on 23 June.

The vote was conducted in a political climate increasingly hostile to immigration and foreigners. We will see how, from the late 1990s, as public opinion began to turn sharply against immigration, fear of the 'other' was ramped up by the media and rarely countered by politicians. Asylum seekers, refugees and migrants from the new members of the European Union in East-Central Europe drew the ire of the press, and aggressive opposition to all forms of migration was ratcheted upwards. The period also saw the emergence of Britain's most successful movement on the far right – the British National Party (BNP). The historic, but nevertheless limited success experienced by a party which can easily be described as neo-fascist acts as an early warning of mistrust of elites, anger over immigration and anxiety towards Britain's changing demography among some sections of the public.

The BNP failed electorally, as all far right parties have done in Britain, but this did not mean the failure of anti-immigration politics. The emergence of the radical right-wing United Kingdom Independence Party (Ukip) during the tenure of the Coalition government and the unprecedented success of such a political party was highly indicative of growing public anger towards the established parties. As David Cameron promised a referendum on Britain's membership of the European Union in 2013, it was indicative of the growing influence of radical right forces. Attempts by the Coalition government to ape the language and politics of Ukip in the hope of stifling the newcomer not only failed, but further dragged British politics rightwards. 2015 saw terrorism and a global refugee crisis arrive at Europe's door, giving the perception of a continent in crisis. When one views the EU referendum in this context, one cannot be shocked by the British public's decision to vote to leave.

The 52 per cent vote reflected a rejection of the established political order by large sections of the public. In many areas, such as the former industrial North, as well as in market and seaside towns in the east of England, the vote to leave the EU was as high as 70 per cent. We will assess local perspectives from the areas which voted to leave in such numbers and in doing so, express the anger and contempt swathes of the public have towards politicians. Finally, we will contextualise the Brexit vote within a wider revolt against the liberal established order in the West.

Brexit is symptomatic of a wider uprising engulfing both Europe and – as shown by the election of Donald Trump as President – the USA. There are striking similarities which cut across national and regional lines, demonstrating that the vote to leave the EU was both a particularly British rebellion and indicative of wider trends rapidly consuming western liberal democracy.

The Brexit vote was not purely against Britain's membership of the European Union. It was a middle finger aimed squarely at the political establishment, who for many had ceased long ago to listen to the concerns of provincial England. It was not based on a cost-benefit analysis of EU membership but on an emotional appeal to the elites for change and a rejection of their cosmopolitan values. And one of the key issues which for many exemplified the contempt the political establishment held for the public, and one of the single biggest issues propelling the Brexit vote, was immigration.

Ninety per cent of people who saw immigration as a drain on the economy voted to leave, as did 88 per cent of those who desired the admittance of fewer immigrants.[1] In a final survey conducted by polling organisation Ipsos MORI one week before the referendum, immigration had surpassed the economy as being the most important issue the electorate would take into account when casting their vote. Fifty-four per cent of likely leave voters stated that immigration was the most important issue guiding their vote.[2] This book will explain how Britain's attitude towards immigration became so hostile.

The Brexit vote reflected a growing and significant divide within British society. It was driven primarily by the groups most at risk of poverty. Sixty-four per cent of the leave vote was from C2DE groups (the lowest socio-economic groups), whereas only 36 per cent from the same groups voted to remain.[3] In particular, the vote reflected stark inequalities in education. Support for Brexit was 30 per cent higher among those whose qualifications were GCSEs or less, than among those with degrees. The vote also revealed a generational divide. Older voters tended to vote for Brexit – the leave vote was 20 per cent higher among those over sixty-five than those aged twenty-five and under.[4]

David Goodhart, former journalist and editor of *Prospect* magazine, speaks of a divide between older, traditional and geographically fixed 'somewheres' and highly educated and mobile 'anywheres'.[5] The vote for Brexit was overwhelmingly driven by the somewheres seeking to 'take back control' from the anywheres. Immigration was seen as providing cultural and economic enrichment for the haves, while the have-nots saw economic competition and a perceived cultural threat. Furthermore, Brexit was an expression of political Englishness. Seventy-nine per cent of Leave voters saw themselves as 'English, rather than British', whereas 60 per cent of Remain voters claimed to be 'British, rather than English'.[6]

Brexit had less to do with economic factors than cultural ones. It has become common to assert that the areas which voted to leave represent those economically 'left behind'. Yet this only gives us part of the picture. We can understand the Brexit vote far better by considering the worldviews of individuals rather than their economic circumstances. Polling conducted by Conservative Party donor and peer Michael Ashcroft released after the referendum vote illustrates this. Respondents were asked whether or not certain subjects were a 'force for ill'. Of all Brexit voters, 81 per cent believed multiculturalism to be a force for ill, social liberalism 80 per cent, immigration 80 per cent, the green movement 78 per cent, feminism 74 per cent, globalisation 69 per cent.[7] Work by Eric Kaufmann, Professor of Politics at Birkbeck

College, University of London has gone even further, showing that values such as opposition to immigration – and, remarkably, favouring the death penalty – are far more effective indicators of a Brexit vote than a low income.[8] This book will seek to map the spread of the illiberal views so integral to the Brexit vote.

Immigration is about more than just people coming into the country. It conjures up debates around race, demographic change and identity. At the end of the Second World War, Britain was an almost uniformly white country. By 1991, around three million non-white people resided in the UK, and by the time of the 2011 census, the figure had more than doubled to seven million – 14 per cent of the total population.[9] Migration from the EU, whilst almost entirely 'white', was nevertheless conflated by politicians and the media with Britain's increasingly multicultural society. A recent study demonstrated that Leavers were concerned more by *non-EU* immigrants than those arriving in Britain under freedom of movement rules.[10] This shows that the Brexit vote was motivated by much wider issues than laws emanating from Brussels.

Yet, until Brexit, there had been precious few successful attempts at mobilising the population against immigration. Something has changed, and attempting to understand what has shifted is a fundamental concern of this book. Key to the task is exploring the failure of political extremism in Britain. Anti-immigrant mobilisations have most often been found on the fringes of mainstream politics. Despite public hostility to immigration, Enoch Powell was never able to break the postwar consensus on the value of immigration, and neither was the extremist National Front. The BNP, whilst more successful, similarly failed to achieve popular support and was treated with the utmost contempt by the very same political commentators in nationalist right-wing tabloids who contributed to its rise.

Within Britain, a consistent anti-fascist consensus has eschewed extremist political *movements*; but, crucially, it has not always suppressed their *ideas*.

Accordingly, what we have seen is the growing *mainstreaming* of far right ideas and their co-option by more centrist political forces. Anti-immigration rhetoric in the public sphere, which stigmatises outsiders as criminals, spongers and a decadent influence on the nation, has become common currency. Many politicians from both the Labour and the Conservative Party sought not to quell, but to ape and adopt the language and policies of anti-immigration demagogues of the past. The rise of Ukip since 2012 and its relatively benign acceptance by the political mainstream (differing from the moral panic which met the rise of the BNP) has been indicative of the fact that nationalist and anti-immigrant ideas are simply no longer taboo. It is a process which has been years in the making, but it reached its apogee during the EU referendum in June 2016.

As Britain entered formal negotiations to leave the European Union almost exactly a year later in June 2017, it was a nation more divided and its politics more unstable than at any point in recent memory. The Brexit vote did not settle the decades-long debate over what Britain's relationship with Europe should be, but opened up a new frontier. The 2017 general election, held amid the horrifying backdrop of three Islamist terror attacks within the space of three months, left an inconclusive result. The country is not merely in a state of flux, but runs the risk of drowning in the Channel. Eschewed by its closest allies abroad following Brexit and bitterly divided at home, the vote to leave the EU was not the end, but merely the beginning. Making sense of how we got here is the chief aim of this book.

English Uprising differs from many other accounts both of

Brexit and of Britain's relationship with the EU. It is primarily historical in focus, aiming to understand the root causes of the Brexit vote, as opposed to providing commentary on the referendum campaign. It does not offer an 'insider' account, but a historical background aimed at demonstrating the long-term and short-term factors involved in the vote to leave. It does not focus solely on the elites who have shaped Britain's relationship with the EU. This 'high-politics' approach, which has characterised much writing on the subject, is inadequate in understanding a vote which had more to do with the British public's revolt against elites, particularly over the issue of immigration, than it did with Britain's historically difficult relationship with Europe.

Evidence for the book's contention – that Brexit was the product of an increasingly toxic and xenophobic British political atmosphere favourable to the radical right – has been gathered through a variety of means. Newspaper archives have been exhaustively plundered, as have sources documenting political discourse, including party pamphlets and speeches. Interviews have been conducted with politicians, both local and national, with a strong local connection to the areas which voted most keenly to leave. Interviews have also been held with academics who can offer expertise on some of the key issues explored in the book: immigration history, populism and the far right.

A brief word on terminology. The book's title refers to 'England' simply due to the fact that a majority in England voted for Brexit, whereas Scotland and Northern Ireland – other constitutive nations of the United Kingdom – did not. Whilst Wales also saw a majority for Brexit, England, as the far larger country, is used out of convenience. The term 'far right' is used throughout to refer to a range of ideologies to the right of mainstream, centre-right politics. According to Cas Mudde, Professor of Political Science at the University of Georgia and world expert on populism, far right is an umbrella term which encompasses predominantly two groups: the radical right and the extreme right. Both groups are nativist, that is, xenophobic and nationalist, and have authoritarian tendencies. The two differ fundamentally however on the crucial issue of democracy: extremists are opposed to democracy, whereas radicals are only against democracy in liberal forms.[11] Put another way, fascists and Nazis are extreme right (and ultimately, a small fringe) whereas Enoch Powell and Ukip are radical right.

The significant discussion devoted to the far right and fascism in this book is not to paint those who voted to leave the EU as extremists. Clearly, not even in their wildest dreams would a fascist movement win over 50 per cent of the vote in Britain. Rather, it is to draw attention to the diversity of anti-immigration politics evident throughout British history on the extreme margins as well as in more centrist forms. The vote to leave does not equate to a vindication of the far right worldview. However, some have tried to paint Leave's victory as having nothing to do with bigotry. As Douglas Carswell, founding member of Vote Leave, unconvincingly argued in April 2017, Brexit was 'not an angry nativist xenophobic vote' but 'won precisely because it was an argument about Britain being open, internationalist, generous, and globalist'. Whilst Brexit was no far right coup d'état, nor was it motivated by the optimistic, global free trade vision held by many on the Vote Leave side.

1
A HISTORY OF INTOLERANCE

Anyway, now the country is ruined. I miss the traditional British way of life, you know before we had the Bulgarians and the Romanians and the Polish and the Russians and the Australians and the Kurdish and the Turkish and the Bengalis and the Pakistanis and the Indians and the West Indians and the Africans and the Huguenots and the Jews and the Normans and the Vikings and the Angles and Saxons and the Romans and the Jutes and those bloody Celts who were first in the door, the foreign fucking idiots, it's been downhill ever since.

Charlie Brooker on *Charlie Brooker's Weekly Wipe*,
Season 2, Episode 1

Throughout the last two centuries, Britain has exhibited a political climate deeply hostile to immigrants. The relatively low number of immigrants entering the country until after the Second World War did not prevent extreme nationalist mobilisations on the far right from scapegoating foreigners as the chief source of Britain's ills. Britons often have an amnesiac view of immigration, which neglects all historical precedent. Be it Commonwealth migration in the 1940s and 50s or migration from Eastern Europe in the twenty-first century, immigration has always tended to be seen as new, different and threatening, and this is something we can witness over decades, if not centuries.

Britain's view of its own history tends to be a rosy one. The crimes committed in its Empire are conveniently forgotten and the xenophobic attitudes which have run through British society for centuries are generally ignored. Margaret Thatcher claimed in a 1988 speech that 'one of the great principles of our Judaic-Christian inheritance is tolerance. People with other faiths and cultures have always been welcomed in our land, assured of equality under the law, of proper respect and of open friendship.'[1] Indeed, according to a recent government guideline aimed at promoting 'British values' at schools, 'tolerance' is alleged to be a trait inherent in the British national character.[2]

Yet we must question the idea that Britain has long been a safe haven for migrants and a tolerant country. As Colin Holmes, Emeritus Professor of History at Sheffield University and an expert on British immigration history since the nineteenth century, told me: 'There's no shortage of evidence of hostility and antipathy towards migrants. To suggest that Britain has been a tolerant country is one of the myths that Britain likes to perpetuate about itself. But it certainly isn't true.'[3] Newcomers have regularly been met with a frosty and, at times, downright hostile welcome from Britons. They have often been marginalised, and in many cases demonised as an unwelcome intrusion. Racism against migrants can be described as a regular feature of responses to immigration, especially in the twentieth century. The relationship between newly arrived migrants and natives is best described as one of tension, which in its most extreme cases has boiled over into outright violence.

By looking at Britain's historical relationship with migration, one can witness many of the similar themes we see today, particularly the hostile response to the arrival of various groups and their scapegoating upon arrival. Immigration has ultimately had a huge impact on Britain's national story and, whilst fraught and unsavoury debates have usually surrounded it, it has been a regular feature of the country's history – both over the past 150 years and prior to that. Migration in the twenty-first century, whilst on a far larger scale than previous waves, cannot be decontextualised from its precedents, and contemporary anti-immigration debates must not be viewed in isolation.

Help wanted: no Irish need apply

Immigration from Ireland to Britain had been common prior to the Great Famine, particularly after the Act of Union in 1800 which had manacled Britain and Ireland together as one country. A wide range of factors would draw people to Britain during this period, whether the desire to escape from the harshness of rural Ireland or the promise of greater opportunities across the Irish Sea. It was, however, the potato blight and the utter desperation it created that would instigate one of the most intense phases of mass migration in British history. In 1841, around four years prior to the Great Famine, approximately 420,000 Irish lived in Britain. Within a decade, this number had nearly doubled to 734,000.[4] Migration was generally concentrated in urban areas – the highest concentrations being in Liverpool, Dundee and Glasgow – which exacerbated the already squalid living conditions prevalent in Britain's cities.

The response of Britons to the new arrivals, particularly in the areas that absorbed most of the Irish, was largely unwelcoming. The Irish were discriminated against in terms of housing and employment. Those with Irish accents were barred from pubs. British workers, themselves subjected to squalid, rat-infested living conditions and low pay, were immediately suspicious of the new competition for jobs. The Irish were blamed for creating stagnation and reductions in wages. Sectarian tension between the Catholic Irish and Protestant British frequently boiled over into outright violence – such as the riots which erupted in Stockport in June 1852, created by local disquiet over Irish migration and the newcomers' open displays of Catholicism. Resentment towards migration followed a similar pattern to the modern day, being expressed both in terms of economic anxiety and cultural chauvinism.

Hostility to Irish migrants was not restricted to localised issues. The national press responded in a hysterical manner not so different from current portrayals of immigration. Take one excerpt from an article in *The Times* in 1847:

> Ireland is pouring into the cities, and even into the villages of this island, a fetid torrent of famine, nakedness, dirt, and fever. Liverpool, whose proximity to Ireland has already procured for it the unhappy distinction of being the most un-healthy town in this island, seems destined to become one of mass disease. The ports of Wales are deliberately invaded by floating pest-houses despatched against them by Irish authorities with the help of English alms.[5]

The British media, politicians and intellectuals ramped up dehumanising depictions of a feral race bearing down on Britain. Prime Minister Benjamin Disraeli had said in 1836, shortly before becoming a Member of Parliament, that the Irish 'hate our order, our civilisation, our enterprising industry, our religion. This wild, reckless, indolent, uncertain and superstitious race have no sympathy with the English character.'[6] Depictions of the Irish as apes were common in English magazine *Punch*. They were held up to be a dirty, unruly, feckless, alcoholic people who could not be trusted. The Victorian age was one in which pseudo-scientific racism was dominant and the Irish were held to be from a lower evolutionary order than the sturdy Anglo-Saxon. Even the Irish love for song, dance and poetry was used as evidence that this was a feeble-minded, childlike people.

As the numbers entering waned towards the end of the nineteenth century, there came a gradual acceptance of the Irish in Britain, who became increasingly integrated. Yet anti-Irish prejudice remained in the country's cultural DNA. In 1921, following the end of hostilities between British and Irish forces in the Irish War of Independence, the majority of Ireland became an independent dominion within the British Empire. This did not stop migration from the Irish Free State, nor did it prevent racialised depictions of the Irish in the media and by intellectuals.

Marginal far right and fascist organisations, such as anti-Jewish publishing group The Britons, continued the trend of portraying the Irish as racially inferior. Economic arguments which held that Irish labour was providing damaging and unnecessary competition as well as driving down wages persisted, as did anti-Catholic sectarianism.[7] Anti-Irish racism has never fully disappeared from Britain, and would reappear during the conflict in Northern Ireland which began in the late 1960s, yet the most overt criticisms eventually became largely restricted to extremists who could never stomach the Irish minority. Another migrant group would receive the brunt of scapegoating in the early twentieth century, as they had done for several decades – the Jews.

The Jewish peril

Jewish immigration to Britain, like that from Ireland, had been driven by desperation and misery. A Jewish presence in Britain had been maintained for centuries before their expulsion by Edward I in 1290, and after their readmission in 1664, a new wave of Jewish migration began in the 1880s. Migrants were overwhelmingly Ashkenazi Jews from Russian Poland, arriving following a series of pogroms and anti-Jewish legislation handed down by the infamously anti-Semitic Tsar Alexander III. Between 1881 and 1914, around 150,000 Jewish settlers arrived in boats from Eastern Europe – many of them illegally or with forged documents.

Whilst mass Jewish migration to Britain had been a recent development, anti-Jewish thought in Britain had a rich history, particularly in popular culture. This predominantly came in the form of Jewish stereotypes such as Shakespeare's Shylock in *The Merchant of Venice* and the conniving Barabas in Christopher Marlowe's *The Jew of Malta*. In both works, Jewish characters are presented as unscrupulous, predatory moneylenders. In the late nineteenth century, Jewish immigrants were seen as a new blight on the British landscape, particularly in their primary area of settlement – east London. Much like the Irish, Jewish immigrants would not be accepted into society for decades and their presence was met with hostility, and in many cases, violence.

Many of the criticisms made of Irish immigrants were applied to Jews a few decades later. Their allegedly 'dirty' appearance was chastised and they were tarnished with the conditions of the slums in which many lived. They were denounced by workers and by some trade union leaders in east London for undercutting the wages of indigenous labour, stealing jobs and straining the already overburdened housing stock. Centuries-old criticisms of Jews as crafty, scheming moneylenders persisted. The seemingly irreconcilable image of the poor eastern European Jew as exploitative capitalist was conjured.

Jewish immigration led to the foundation of 'anti-alien' organisations such as the British Brothers League, founded in 1902. The BBL, which claimed to have a membership of 45,000 (although in reality the figure was probably much smaller than this), acted as a lobby group for the restriction of immigration. At rallies, BBL speakers bellowed that Britain was becoming 'the dumping ground for the scum of Europe'.[8] Following the activities of the League and others, Jewish immigration would lead to legislation which set a precedent for government control over immigration.

The Aliens Act of 1905 was the first item of legislation in peacetime British history introduced to restrict immigration. It specifically sought to keep out poor, homeless and diseased migrants; an 'alien' would be prevented from entering the country 'if he cannot show that he has in his possession . . . the means of decently supporting himself and his dependents . . . if he is a lunatic or an idiot, or owing to any disease of infirmity liable to become a charge upon the public rates . . . if he has been sentenced in a foreign country with which there is an extradition treaty for a crime'.[9]

David Feldman, Professor of History at Birkbeck College, University of London and Director of the Pears Institute for the Study of Anti-Semitism, argues that the 1905 Aliens Act marks a turning point in Britain's history of immigration in that, from 1905, 'immigration was regarded as a problem.' Prior to that, 'immigration was seen, by some people, as a problem, but it wasn't the state's problem' and was largely managed through civil organisations. The 1905 Act was in fact relatively lax in comparison to the immigration control imposed (by means of the 1914 Alien Restrictions Act) following the outbreak of the First World War, and maintained after 1918. The Home Office subsequently sought to turn Britain into 'a country of zero immigration and immigration laws against "alien" immigrants were extremely tight'.[10]

Left-wing upheavals in the former monarchies destroyed by the First World War, colonial uprisings and widespread conspiracy theories made the world seem a more dangerous place for the ruling class. Although the population of Jews in Britain was minuscule, this would not stop the scapegoating of Jews and the running of campaigns directed against foreigners. This activity was principally orchestrated on the fringes of politics as well as on the hard right 'Die Hard' wing of the Conservative Party. The period between the two world wars would ultimately be one in which radical right-wing politics defined the age in Europe, and Britain was not immune.

The origins of the far right

The origins of the contemporary far right can be located in the early post-First World War period. The conclusion of the deadliest war in human history in 1918 gave birth to a new political extremism on the right in Europe, and Britain was no exception. The most fundamental features of this sea-change in right-wing politics have been maintained until this day. Whilst Britain had been on the winning side, the war, which had led to human destruction on a previously unknown scale, had installed in many on the traditional conservative right a great pessimism about Britain and its Empire. Jews became heavily associated, even in mainstream circles, with subversive and revolutionary movements, especially Communism. Winston Churchill wrote in 1920:

> There is no need to exaggerate the part played in the creation of Bolshevism and in the actual bringing about of the Russian Revolution by these international and for the most part atheistical Jews. It is certainly a very great one; it probably outweighs all others. With the notable exception of Lenin, the majority of the leading figures are Jews . . . there are many non-Jews every whit as bad as the worst of the Jewish revolutionaries, the part played by the latter in proportion to their numbers in the population is astonishing.[11]

Comments such as these from Churchill are illustrative of a post war climate ripe for a nationalist backlash in British politics. The Bolshevik Revolution of 1917 in Russia and the perceived rise of Communism across Europe had provoked terror amongst the traditional establishment (including the royal family) of a new anti-capitalist, anti-Christian force which threatened to infect Britain's vast labour movement and challenge the country's imperial interests in Asia. More importantly, the Irish War of Independence between 1919 and 1921 (leading to independence for five-sixths of Ireland) had given rise to the idea of a British Empire in rapid decline. The early 1920s reflected the beginning of a new imperialist, xenophobic, anti-socialist political creed in Britain. At the most extreme end of the spectrum are fascists and Nazis, the dominant strand of the far right during the interwar period. Professor Matthew Feldman, Co-Director of the Centre for Fascist, Anti-Fascist and Post-Fascist Studies at Teesside University, argues that fascism is a 'religious conception of politics', one which values 'homogeneity' and seeks to 'push class distinctions into the background in favour of ethnic and cultural ties'. It is a revolutionary ideology which 'prides itself on creating a new order'.[12]

Fascism would first emerge in Italy following the crisis which beset the country after the First World War. Many in Britain initially thought positively of the radical nationalist Mussolini's rise to power and his subsequent crushing of left-wing political opposition. Fascism was first imported into Britain, albeit manacled with traditional conservatism, in 1923 with the founding of the British Fascisti. The BF, whilst achieving a not insignificant membership of around 30,000 (the vast majority of whom however were not active members), were never a force to be reckoned with in British politics – never participating in a general election and having less than a handful of councillors elected.

The ideology of the BF reflected a new, authoritarian, anti-Communist political movement which also absorbed traditional Tory 'Die Hard' ideas of British imperialism and related white racial supremacism. Their outlook on the world was utterly conspiratorial – seeing 'Bolshevik' conspiracies in every corner of the globe who sought to stir up unrest in Britain's colonies. The 'hidden hand' of Bolshevism (which was held to be strongly influenced by Jewry) was alleged by the BF to be practically everywhere – in the Labour Party and trade unions, among Irish republicans, in Gandhi's Indian National Congress.

The interwar far right's outlook on politics was deeply paranoid and based on conspiracy theory which merged anti-Semitism with anti-Communism, and is best located in the work of writer Nesta Webster. Despite a promising but brief stint as a historian, Webster would pen a number of works of conspiracy theory which argued that every revolutionary movement – from the French Revolution to Bolshevism – was directed by German Freemasons and the Illuminati. She railed against 'subversive' movements such as socialism which she claimed sought to smash traditional Christian, monarchist and conservative values. She saw the British Empire as having fallen under grave peril from subversion, orchestrated by a powerful, shadowy elite, and believed that fascism could root out the subversive menace.

As was typical of the radical right, Webster believed in a global Jewish conspiracy which had been growing in power since the late nineteenth century, arguing that 'behind Freemasonry, behind even the secret societies that made of Freemasons their adepts, another power was making itself felt, a power that ever since the Congress of Wilhelmsbad in 1782 had been slowly gaining ground – the power of the *Jews*'.[13] Webster had many high-profile fans, including one Winston Churchill, who had read her works on the French Revolution, where she documented alleged infiltration of revolutionary movements by clandestine forces.

Anti-Semitic conspiracy theories ran through the British far right, as playwright and anti-fascist writer David Edgar notes, 'like Blackpool runs through rock'.[14] Perhaps one of the most extreme anti-Semites during the interwar period, a man who would also greatly influence the more extreme elements of the postwar far right, was Arnold Leese.

Leese began his political career in the BF, but soon left due to their failure to adopt a more extreme fascist ideology. He came to lead another fascist organisation – the Imperial Fascist League (IFL). As Adolf Hitler rose to prominence in Weimar Germany, Leese developed a fanatical devotion to him and in particular, to the Nazis' strand of biological racism and anti-Semitism.

Leese blamed every conceivable political phenomenon on Jews. But the IFL, who were active throughout the 1930s and strongly influenced by Hitler's National Socialists, were even less successful than the BF – achieving membership in the low hundreds. Both organisations' obsession with conspiracies – the idea of secret Communist activity seeking to destroy the British Empire and Jews controlling world finance – would significantly distance them from the mainstream of British politics. It is not dismissive to argue that the vast majority of Britons had probably never heard of either group.

One political mobilisation of extreme nationalism, which eclipsed the BF and IFL and has unquestionably left its mark on British history, is former Labour Party minister Sir Oswald Mosley's black-shirted British Union of Fascists, founded in 1932. Mosley sought to do away with what he called the 'old gang' of democratic British politicians in favour of a centrally planned, modern and highly autocratic state with himself as supreme leader – a plan closely modelled on the system of Fascist Italy.

Mosleyite fascism was different from that of the BF and IFL. Mosley was a self-described socialist who had supported the General Strike of 1926 – which saw nearly two million workers strike in a dispute over coal miners' pay – and was an early advocate of high levels of government spending and investment in industry. Whilst his background was aristocratic, he sought to animate the working class around economically nationalist and protectionist policies (such as the restriction and banning of imports from abroad) which would enhance British manufacturing. At first, it seemed as though Mosley was succeeding. In 1934, eighteen months after the founding of the BUF, its membership had reached 40,000 and it had gained some high-profile supporters, including Lord Rothermere, proprietor of the *Daily Mail*. Rothermere's backing led to the now infamous headline 'Hurrah for the Blackshirts!', emblazoned on the front of the paper in January 1934.

Despite having a substantial political programme designed by the cerebral Mosley and his followers, the BUF were never able to shed their violent image. Their April 1934 rally at Olympia, west London, is often cited as the moment British fascism's violent nature was exposed. As Mosley addressed the thousands-strong crowd, protesters who had arrived to heckle were violently ejected by fascist thugs and the ensuing hostilities were widely publicised. What was probably more damning, however, was the occurrence just over two months later in Germany of what became known as the 'night of the long knives'. This bloody event, which saw Hitler's SS troops execute dozens of political enemies and imprison hundreds more, including long-term ally and paramilitary *Sturmabteilung* (SA) leader Ernst Röhm, was splashed across the British newspapers and instantaneously tainted the fascist brand with violence and murder.

Despite a collapse in membership in the second half of 1934, the BUF gave up all pretence of respectability and turned to the streets. They intensified their anti-Semitic rhetoric and violent fascist shock troops ran riot, particularly around London's East End. Communist Party meetings were violently disrupted and counter-demonstrations at fascist meetings dealt with viciously. In addition, the BUF increasingly became openly anti-Semitic throughout the 1930s – provoking violence against British Jews (many of whom lived in the East End) as well as expounding the idea of a vast Jewish conspiracy that sought to destroy the British nation.

The BUF's director of propaganda, former theatre critic A.K. Chesterton, who would go on to form the National Front in 1967, spoke of the 'reeking corruption of the Jew' and described them as a 'jackal race'.[15] Another infamous and anti-Semitic Mosleyite was William Joyce, better known as 'Lord Haw-Haw'. Joyce would escape to Nazi Germany before the authorities could reach him in 1940 and spend the rest of the war acting as a propagandist on German radio, before being captured by British troops and hanged for treason in 1946. Mosley has often been portrayed as a reluctant anti-Semite, pushed into it by others. However, he regularly blamed Jews for the impoverished state of much of Britain, citing 'the forces of international Jewish finance used to sweat the working classes'.[16]

The BUF, like many in British establishment circles, not only looked favourably towards Adolf Hitler's Nazi regime in Germany, but were strongly in favour of appeasement during the second half of the 1930s. They protested vigorously against confrontation with Germany as Hitler took first Austria, then Czechoslovakia. When war was declared in September 1939, it was clear that the days of fascists in Britain were numbered, but it was only at the end of the 'phoney war' in May 1940 when hundreds of active fascists, including Mosley, were rounded up by the government and interned under Defence Regulation 18B. Fascists' support for Mussolini and then Hitler had led the government to believe that they might represent a fifth column capable of sabotaging Britain's war for survival against Nazi Germany. Fascists – those who claimed to be Britain's staunchest patriots – would spend Britain's 'finest hour' locked away for fear of subversion.

One might assume, perhaps naively, that the Second World War, where the British Empire took on totalitarian Nazi Germany and its fascist allies at the cost of nearly 400,000 lives, would lead to the death of fascism and radical nationalism in Britain.

Yet many of the British fascists imprisoned during the Second World War resumed their activities shortly after their release. It could be argued that the conditions of the interwar period were as favourable as they were ever going to be for the far right, with an economic depression and the perception that there were 'successful' fascist and authoritarian governments on the continent. Yet the conspiratorial worldview of fascists, their extreme ideas and authoritarian nature were always seen as eccentric by most.

The postwar far right would find it even harder than before the war to establish their ideas. Matthew Feldman describes the post-Second World War climate as extremely hostile and explains why fascists rarely called themselves by that name after 1945: 'every ideology changes and develops with time and for fascism, the key element was recognising the stigma of 1945; the World War and genocide. This is why you find precious few fascists after the war calling themselves "fascists".'[7] Britons had just spent the past five years fighting fascism at an astronomical cost, both in terms of money and lives – they were unlikely to be inclined to vote for it.

Yet the far right reared its ugly ahead almost immediately after the end of hostilities. The most notable extremist organisation which emerged following the end of the Second World War was the British League of Ex-Servicemen (BLXS). Led by interwar BUF member and 18B detainee Jeffrey Hamm, the BLXS were highly anti-Semitic and sought to terrorise the streets of east London as the BUF had done in the 1930s. They also saw the political climate as favourable to their anti-Jewish ideas. British imperial control in the Mandate of Palestine was crumbling and Zionist terrorist organisations were engaging in increasingly violent and deadly activities in order to achieve their dream of a Jewish state.

The peak of this activity came in July 1946 when the Irgun (a Zionist paramilitary organisation) bombed the King David Hotel in Jerusalem, killing ninety-one people, including many British officials. The 'Sergeants Affair' occurred a year later, when two British soldiers were murdered and their booby-trapped and bloodied corpses publicly displayed hanging from a eucalyptus tree. Several anti-Jewish riots were witnessed around the country, and the rhetoric of the BLXS at their east London rallies became even more extreme. At one point, an activist, linking British Jews with those in Palestine, called for 'a cleansing campaign', arguing that 'we want to cleanse the British country and the British Empire for good and all time of the alien filth and the scum and the traitors that reside here in this country'.[18]

The BLXS joined with Oswald Mosley shortly afterwards, in 1948, when Mosley founded the Union Movement, an organisation practically indistinguishable from his interwar BUF. One key distinction was his curious embrace of European unity, which he saw as essential if European imperial powers were to maintain their African colonies and the continent was to hold its own in the face of Soviet and US power. The violently anti-Semitic rhetoric of the BLXS was curbed, yet Mosley still launched attacks on Jews, despite ever-increasing evidence of their attempted extermination by the Nazis in Europe.

Mosley regularly sought to use events in Palestine as a means of attacking Jews and relativising Nazi crimes. Why, he argued, was violence 'accepted when advanced by Jews and subject to world condemnation and a war of extermination when put forward by Germans?'[19] It became increasingly clear that many on the far right were not only indifferent to the plight of the Jews during the Second World War, but sceptical of whether it had really happened at all.

This disturbing history of fascism, anti-Semitism and extremism may seem a world away from Britain's current politics, even the Brexit referendum. Yet it is important for a number of reasons. First, it is a fact that nationalist, xenophobic political mobilisations most often find themselves on the right-wing fringes – much like the anti-immigration politics of today. Crude anti-Semitism and racist language has gradually become unacceptable, and movements on the right have become adept at political communication which is less openly bigoted. Public displays of racism are not just socially taboo in Britain any more but often illegal. Many of the same underlying bigotries exist, yet Britain's political culture has demonstrably shifted. This history of fascism ultimately opens a window to anti-immigration politics during a period where standards of acceptable political discourse are radically different.

The postwar period saw a radical transformation in British politics and society, and in the economic system which underpinned them. Of most interest to us is the fact that Britain became a truly multicultural and multiracial society. Previously, racial problems had largely existed in faraway colonies, where white rule and dominance was near absolute. The extent to which Britain's perceptions of race derive solely from the colonial experience has been debated by historians, but one cannot argue with the fact that when non-white migrants began arriving in the late 1940s, white Britons generally saw themselves as superior. The advent of large-scale Commonwealth immigration after the Second World War was not the first time the British and other races had come into contact – far from it – but it was the first time black, Asian and white British were to live side by side theoretically as equal citizens.

The Empire comes to Britain

The most significant migration to Britain since the Jewish immigration of the late nineteenth century came in the late 1940s. Between the early 1950s and 1983, however, more people actually *emigrated* from Britain, largely to Australia, than arrived in almost every year. Whilst many more left the country than arrived, concerns were not so much about the balance of numbers entering and leaving, but specifically about those coming in. The decades which followed the Second World War have thus almost universally been characterised as a period of mass *immigration*. This is in large part due to the visibly changing ethnic make-up of British society and the true beginnings of a diverse, multicultural nation.

Following wartime hero Winston Churchill's unceremonious dumping from office in the 1945 general election, Clement Attlee and the Labour Party were elected on a platform of mass reconstruction of infrastructure and investment in industry. In order to address a chronic labour shortage, workers from the Commonwealth were encouraged to come to Britain through the British Nationality Act of 1948, and many jumped at the chance for work and a new life in the imperial metropole. The first to come were largely West Indian, and by 1958 around 115,000 had arrived from the Caribbean. In addition, over 50,000 came from former British India – now the independent states of India and Pakistan. This figure would rise significantly during the 1960s and 1970s, as the workforce of Britain's factories swelled with manual workers from the Indian subcontinent.

White Britons' response to the policy was fierce and the

decades which followed would be fraught with racial tension, bitterness and, in the worst cases, violence. Politicians sought to maintain order and at times to stick up for the rights of migrants, yet they were ultimately trapped within a prison of public opinion which demanded strict controls. The postwar period marks the first time that mass immigration met with mass democracy, a tension which has never truly been resolved.

Many working-class communities in which the migrants settled did not take well to their new neighbours. Discrimination against black migrants in their search for jobs and housing was widespread among many areas of settlement, particularly Notting Hill in west London. Colour bars and segregation existed in dancehalls and pubs, which sought to refuse entry to blacks. As with new arrivals in the past, negative stereotypes of newcomers were rampant.

This was particularly the case with those black migrants, to whom most of Britain's exposure had come through a profoundly racist imperial lens which held that black people were lazy, untrustworthy savages with a voracious sexual appetite. This was not helped by the Kenyan Emergency, which began in 1952, and during which gruesome acts by the mysterious Mau Mau were sensationally reported by the British press.[20] A survey conducted at the time discovered that over two-thirds of Britons had a low opinion of black people. Some saw blacks as

heathens who practised head-hunting, cannibalism, infanticide, polygamy and 'black magic'. They saw them as uncivilised, backward people, inherently inferior to Europeans, living in primitive mud huts 'in the bush', wearing few clothes, eating strange foods, and suffering from unpleasant diseases. They saw them as ignorant and illiterate, speaking strange languages, and lacking proper education.[21]

Despite the obvious demand for workers, immigrants would be criticised for undercutting wages and taking others' jobs. Trade unions were often deeply hostile to black migrants and demonstrated ambivalence to the racism and discrimination suffered by black and Asian workers. This attitude followed a general pattern which expressed concern over immigration chiefly in terms of its impact on white Britons. Whilst no legislation to curb migration would appear until 1962, many politicians were already becoming deeply concerned by the impact of immigration and the political backlash it was likely to cause. In 1954, Winston Churchill expressed his concern to Jamaican Governor, Sir Hugh Foot, over Britain turning into a 'magpie society . . . that will never do'.[22]

In the late 1950s, nearly 100,000 Caribbean people alone resided in London. More often than not, they found themselves in impoverished areas such as Notting Hill. Poverty was a fact of life not just for the local black population, but also for the white working class – who viewed the new arrivals from the Caribbean as competitors for housing and services. Violence and intimidation towards the black community, whilst always present, grew during the 1950s – the instigators often being far-right racists, as well as the working-class yobs known as 'Teddy Boys' (due to their unique Edwardian-style dress), who sought to intimidate black people and vandalise their property. Tension between West Indian migrants and Britons in Notting Hill boiled over into an all-out riot in the early hours of 30 August 1958, following a spate of violent attacks on black residents that month by white people, including Teddy Boys and the far right.

Crowds of youths in their hundreds chased and attacked black residents. Molotov cocktails, knives and bats were used, and houses occupied by blacks were pelted with milk bottles. The Caribbean community fought back, for the most part, entirely in self-defence. When the police managed to restore order after a week of violence, dozens of the white instigators were arrested, as were some of those from the black community who had been attacked. Whilst the most extreme violence had been stopped, community tension lasted for months. In one tragic case, over ten months after the riots, Kelso Cochrane – a recent arrival from the Caribbean – was set upon by a gang of white men and stabbed to death with a stiletto knife in a racist attack.

The Notting Hill riots of 1958 have regularly been attributed to far right activities, a sign of the continued presence of fascism after the war. Yet, whilst there was certainly an element of far right activism in the riots, racist acts were largely conducted by those not connected to the far right. Dr Joe Mulhall, Senior Researcher at HOPE not Hate and an expert on postwar British fascism, argues: 'In some senses the far right has been used as a scapegoat. It has become a comfortable position to say "the reason that these racist things happen is because committed activists are racist and active fascists". The resulting effect is that it takes the heat off the wider society, because it is easier to think of a society as progressive, modern, welcoming and inclusive and there is a little group of fascists that cause these problems. That's much more comfortable.'

However, Mulhall goes on to argue, 'If you look at the fifties and the reaction when people first arrived, speak to the West Indians themselves or you look at sources produced at the time, the reaction to them was incredibly hostile, incredibly racist.

Both at a governmental level and all the way through wider society, whether it was in housing, getting jobs, etc. It was a much more broad issue than just a small group of racists.'

Mulhall also argues against overemphasising the role played by the far right in the wider racism of postwar Britain: 'It is much easier when things like the Notting Hill riots happen, or more general responses to West Indian immigration, to say that these problems were caused by a small group of fascists or far right activists than to actually accept what was happening.' Their impact, he says, was in fact minimal. Racism was endemic rather than limited to a fringe.

Furthermore, even the far right had not recognised the salience of immigration: 'If you look at the fascist press itself in the 1950s, they are far more preoccupied with other issues such as anti-Semitism and anti-Communism. There is then a tactical shift in the mid-1950s, when they start to see that such widespread prejudice towards this issue, that it might be something that will play.' Ultimately, 'it starts to change when they see political capital in it'.[23] The far right never understood the importance of the issue of immigration until more mainstream forces had already adopted it.

The surrender of an Empire

The Conservative Party, led by Winston Churchill, was returned to government in 1951 after a six-year absence. The far right in the early 1950s consisted of several very small and eccentric organisations. In 1953, A.K. Chesterton, formerly the BUF's so-called Director of Propaganda, founded the League of Empire Loyalists (LEL). The LEL repudiated much of the authoritarianism of interwar British fascism, and Chesterton, one of the few fascists not to be interned and to fight in the war, expressed his disgust at Nazi war crimes. The LEL nevertheless reflected a continuation of the nationalist, xenophobic, conspiratorial and occasionally violent politics of the 1930s. As the world increasingly discovered, to its horror, the scale and nature of the Nazi genocide of European Jewry, the LEL and other far right organisations held steadfastly to anti-Semitism within their political programme and to a belief in a global Jewish conspiracy – now located in the recently founded state of Israel – as a malevolent force seeking to undermine and destroy what remained of British world power.

Chesterton's LEL dominated far right politics during the 1950s. An organisation of around 3,000 active members, they were distraught by the rapid diminution of British imperial power. Whilst many were traditional conservatives, others also subscribed fully to Chesterton's prolific anti-Jewish conspiracy theory writings. John Tyndall, future chairman of the National Front and founder of the BNP, would receive his political tutelage from Chesterton in the LEL. Remarking decades later on his time in the party and demonstrating the importance of bizarre conspiracy theories to the far right, Tyndall remarked: 'The biggest contribution Chesterton made to my thinking was in the development of an understanding of the conspiracy theory of history.'[24] Martin Webster, who would also lead the National Front, was another member, as was Colin Jordan – a peculiar figure who would become the guiding star of Britain's neo-Nazi movement.

The majority of the LEL's membership was aptly described by one historian as 'more colonel blimpish, than fascist'.[25] In practice, it acted as a radical right-wing fringe group which coalesced around the Tory right. One of the most remarkable features of the LEL was its attachment to political stunts and madcap demonstrations, designed to gain media coverage. This included anything from throwing pig entrails at Kenyan nationalist leader Jomo Kenyatta on a visit to Britain, to popping up from under the stage during Conservative Party conference speeches to criticise the government over its handling of the British Empire.

The far right were at this point slightly madcap and marginal to the debate. Jewish conspiracies would have seemed positively bonkers to the majority who came across them. The LEL's Edwardian attachment to the British Empire demonstrated that it was entirely stuck in the past. Decolonisation, a tragedy for many ruling elites, never really inflamed the British population, who were indifferent to Empire. The far right had not yet understood the potency of anti-immigration politics in postwar Britain. Most importantly, Britain was still living in the wake of the Second World War and Nazi Germany – an experience which shaped, and continues to shape, the nation's conscience. Overt political displays of racism conjured up images of Hitler.

An anti-fascist patriotism was fresh in the minds of many following the Second World War and the vast majority were appalled at the return of the far right. However, Britain's wartime experiences and the anti-fascist culture which subsequently developed sat easily with the negative backlash towards Commonwealth immigration. Joe Mulhall argues: 'There is a fundamental difference between anti-fascism and anti-racism. There has always been racism in Britain. The opposition to Nazism and fascism doesn't mean that many people weren't simultaneously racist. Being anti-fascist does not necessarily equate to being progressive.' He argues that 'pride in winning the war did not necessarily translate in lots of people's minds into being open to black immigration'.[26] The ground, whilst not ripe for a postwar far right revival, was not inhospitable to it either.

We see, then, that prior to the Second World War, Britain did not need many immigrants for there to be a small but noteworthy nationalist backlash and far right movement. Prior to 1948 and the arrival of migrants from the Commonwealth, Britain was an almost entirely white country. Its foreign-born population was a minuscule proportion of the whole. This is significant to today's events as it demonstrates that the rise of nationalism and intolerant, xenophobic ideas is not merely a retort to uncontrolled immigration. To blame Brexit on unprecedentedly high levels of migration is to miss the point entirely. Aggressive nationalism and nativism is not merely responsive to wider events but has shown to be a regular feature throughout British history, regardless of the number of immigrants. The demographic change which came from Commonwealth immigration following the Second World War merely exacerbated an existing political current. It is to that change that we will now turn.

2

BRITAIN'S MULTIRACIAL SOCIETY
AND THE FAILURE OF EXTREMISM

There is a limit to the number of (and I'm going to use this word in an entirely neutral sense) aliens who can be brought into a nation, particularly as close-knit and concentrated a nation as Britain is, without breaking the bonds of that society and setting up intolerable frictions and stresses as damaging to one side as to the other. Now, this is a question of number. But the relationship between number and difference is clearly important, because the more different they are – and colour is a signal, an outward signal of differences (not significant in itself, but it signalises other differences that one can't deny) – the greater the difference, the smaller the numbers that can at any one time be accepted without breaking, or being thought to break (which comes to the same thing if we're talking about psychology), the framework of a nation and a society. So it's numbers.

Enoch Powell, speaking on *The Firing Line*
with William F. Buckley, 19 May 1969

A poll conducted after the Notting Hill riots in 1958 indicates that whilst public negativity towards non-white immigration had not yet become highly pronounced, attitudes were hardening. Only 9 per cent of those surveyed blamed the black community for the riots, and a relatively meagre 16 per cent wished to see restrictions on coloured immigration. However, 54 per cent did not believe in equal access to council housing, whilst 37 per cent opposed equal opportunities for jobs. A mere 2 per cent backed the relaxed Commonwealth immigration system. More tellingly, people's perceptions of migrant communities appear to have become more negative – 30 per cent stated that they would consider moving if a non-white person moved next door, and only 13 per cent approved of interracial marriages (71 per cent disapproved).[1]

The disturbances at Notting Hill, as well as public disquiet over immigration, ultimately drove the government towards imposing controls on migrants. Given the fact that such controls had a disproportionate impact on non-whites, it is not difficult to view this as a racist policy. Indeed, a matter of days after the riots, the Marquess of Salisbury (formerly Minister for Colonial Relations) showed he was in favour of an immigration policy determined by race, stating that he was 'extremely apprehensive about the economic and social results, for Europeans and Africans alike, that were likely to flow following an unrestricted immigration of men and women of African race into Britain'.[2]

David Feldman told me that 'there was the view that people of colour were different. That went from the top of society to the bottom. It's no coincidence that what came about to regulate that was a raft of legislation that was discussed as "race relations". Race wasn't thought of as a construct; it was thought of as a real thing which had to be regulated.' He argues that the end of Empire had exacerbated the problem: 'the "people that we once ruled over there were now over here, and we didn't rule them over there any more". There was a world turned upside down aspect to it' which required state intervention. The bi-partisan consensus which emerged and was largely followed by successive Conservative and Labour governments was that immigration and racial issues should be 'regulated by a mixture of immigration restriction and race relations legislation. Politicians who tried to break through that consensus, most notably Enoch Powell and his supporters, were marginalised.'[3]

Take back control

The 1960s tends to be seen as the golden age of social liberalism in Britain, when the country finally threw off the shackles of Victorian morality and embraced pop music, drugs and free love. Yet in terms of immigration, Colin Holmes says, 'the 1960s is a decisive decade. Although you get the first Race Relations Acts which tried to control discrimination, you do get immigration controls.'[4] The decade saw the institutionalisation of anti-immigration politics in the UK, beginning with the Commonwealth Immigrants Act of 1962.

By the autumn of 1961, around 300,000 new migrants had arrived within a decade. Unrest over the growing impact of immigration led to the 1962 Act, introduced by the Conservative government led by Harold Macmillan. The Act represented the first of a series of attempts by postwar British governments to demonstrate that they could control immigration. It is important to note that when there was conflict between migrants and the native population (such as in the Notting Hill riots), immigration was largely deemed to be the problem, as opposed to racism or the prejudices of the British. Legislation which criminalised discrimination against migrants on the grounds of race was yet to appear.

The Act was the first of several explicitly designed to restrict the 'coloured' migration which had begun in the late 1940s. A quota system for unskilled immigration, which targeted Commonwealth migrants from the West Indies and South Asia, was introduced in tandem with a voucher system for those with jobs lined up or who could offer specialised skills. The Act also authorised the British government to deport Commonwealth migrants convicted of certain offences punishable by incarceration. It did not address family reunification and permitted the immigration of wives, children under working age and partners of both current and future immigrants. Bitterly opposed by Labour, with leader Hugh Gaitskell describing it as 'cruel and brutal anti-colour legislation', it was similarly condemned by the Prime Minister of the Federation of the West Indies, Sir Grantley Adams, who likened it to South Africa's apartheid policies:

> West Indians are firmly convinced that by this action Britain has begun to take steps which are no different in kind to the basis on which the system of apartheid in South Africa is based . . . it is inconceivable that West Indians who form less than one half of one per cent of the population of Great Britain can constitute any threat to Britain's economy or health. There has been no evidence to indicate that West Indians are less law-abiding or moral than the people of Britain whose beliefs in law, freedom and justice they share . . . It will in future be difficult for any person from the Commonwealth to accept unreflectingly [sic] the oft-repeated assertion of multi-racial partnership.[5]

Opinion polls, however, showed that the Act had 70 per cent support and only 13 per cent opposition. The vast majority of respondents appeared not to be personally affected by immigration: only 13 per cent said there were 'many' immigrants where they lived and worked.[6] And there were further indications that the public was adopting an ever-toughening stance on immigration. There was anxiety over the influx of non-whites entering the country and competing for resources, and the government had appeared to confirm that this was a problem through their imposition of immigration controls. During the second half of the 1960s, the number of people polled who saw non-white immigration as a 'very serious social problem' began to rise. In 1965, a significant 55 per cent held this view, reaching a high in 1969, with a substantial 69 per cent.[7] Also during this period, few appeared to see any benefits to immigration and viewed it as having 'harmed' the country. In 1965 a mere 16 per cent believed immigration from the Commonwealth had benefited Britain, whereas 52 per cent thought it had caused harm. The idea that immigration 'harmed' Britain only became more widespread, being held by 61 per cent in 1968.[8]

An indication of the growing salience and potency of anti-immigration politics was witnessed during the election of Peter Griffiths as Conservative Member of Parliament for the Birmingham seat of Smethwick in 1964. Smethwick had been a Labour seat since 1918 and the party saw a national swing in their favour at the 1964 general election, bringing in a Labour government for the first time since 1951. Whilst Smethwick had not actually experienced the high levels of immigration of its neighbouring West Midlands constituencies, it was a hot issue in local politics.

The local Conservative Party had been arguing strongly against immigration prior to the election and had been making significant electoral inroads on the issue. Despite the Labour Party's return to government that year, there was a significant swing away from Labour in Smethwick, as headmaster and local politician Griffiths defeated Labour Shadow Foreign Secretary Patrick Gordon Walker on a quite vicious anti-immigrant platform. The ugly campaign was typified by the now infamous campaign slogan: 'If you want a nigger for a neighbour, vote Labour'.[9]

Whilst Griffiths denied any responsibility for the leaflet, he nevertheless refused to criticise it, stating, 'I should think that is a manifestation of popular feeling. I would not condemn anyone who said that.'[10] Upon his election, Labour Prime Minister Harold Wilson said Griffiths would be treated like a 'parliamentary leper' (and in doing so, instigated uproar in the Commons chamber), and he was defeated at the general election just two years later. Griffiths had been quarantined by the mainstream. Enoch Powell, soon to replace Griffiths as Britain's anti-immigrant rabblerouser-in-chief, nevertheless noted how effectively he had utilised anti-immigrant sentiment for political gain. Just days after Griffiths' election, Powell said: 'I do not agree with people who say that the result is a disgrace.'[11]

Wilson's Labour government, despite their opposition to the 1962 Act, found themselves once in power not just going along with a growing consensus that immigration must be strictly controlled, but implementing further restrictions. They tightened controls in 1965 and the number of work vouchers available was cut. Public opinion strongly favoured such measures: 87 per cent agreed with the government's action to strictly control immigration.[12] However, recognising the hostility of the public towards immigration, they also introduced the Race Relations Act of 1965, designed to outlaw racial discrimination against immigrants.

In 1968, another Act was introduced by Labour to control immigration from the Commonwealth. It was a direct response to the recently independent Kenya's 'Africanisation' policy implemented by President Jomo Kenyatta, which pushed Asians who had arrived in the country during the colonial era out of jobs in government and industry. Many Asians in Kenya had taken up the option of British citizenship following the country's independence in 1963 and were exempt from the 1962 Act. The Commonwealth Immigrants Act of 1968, hastily constructed in time to prevent a 'rush' of thousands of desperate migrants from Kenya, stated that immigration was only possible for those with a parent or grandparent born in Britain or for those holding British citizenship. It was roundly supported by both parties and reflected increasingly stringent immigration controls.

A 1967 poll provides indications of the main reasons for opposition to immigration. The poll, conducted by Gallup, asked respondents to choose what they thought to be the 'main causes of any opposition to coloured people immigrating to this country'. Forty-nine per cent believed opposition was due to the perception that immigrants were supported by welfare, 41 per cent thought it was due to them congregating 'in a neighbourhood and turning it into a slum'; 36 per cent believed it was due to immigrants having 'different habits and customs', whilst 30 per cent said it was because they took jobs from the British.[13] A range of concerns was expressed, relating to economic, social and cultural factors.

Prior to 1968, there had been strong indications of the potency of anti-immigration politics. Governments had sought to meet the demands of the public by demonstrating that immigration could and would be controlled. Yet, for many, 'control' was not enough. Many wanted a reversal of the ethnic change Britain had witnessed in just under two decades. The prospect of a return to a white Britain did not seem impossible at this point. The far

right in particular sought to manipulate anti-immigration sentiment for their own, sinister purposes, but achieved little success
even at a local level. More mainstream but nevertheless hard
right organisations such as the Monday Club – led by a rump of
Tory MPs – railed about the threat non-white immigration posed
to the British nation and the need, at the very least, to halt it. Yet
the name of one man would go down in history as having the
most combustible impact on immigration politics: John Enoch
Powell.

Enoch Powell and the English backlash

Few figures have had a bigger impact on debates surrounding
immigration in Britain than Enoch Powell. Powell ignited the
immigration debate in the late 1960s and his legacy is almost
as evident today. His life prior to his rise to notoriety almost
exclusively for his stance on immigration was nothing less than
remarkable. Born in 1912 in Birmingham to lower middle class
parents, Powell would eventually achieve a Double Star First
in Latin and Greek at Trinity College, Cambridge. He became
Professor of Greek at Sydney University aged twenty-five, before
enthusiastically joining the military as the Second World War
loomed. His rise in the military would be similarly impressive –
making the surge from private to brigadier.

Despite having ambitions to become Viceroy of India, Powell
would instead embark on a parliamentary career spanning more
than thirty-seven years after he was elected as Conservative MP
for Wolverhampton South West in 1950. He would serve in the
cabinet for just over three years in Harold Macmillan's government between 1960 and 1963 as Health Secretary (while holding

the post, incidentally, Powell spent much of his time encouraging nurses from the Commonwealth to work in the NHS). An early advocate of the Thatcherite doctrine of monetarism, Powell would have a huge influence on Britain's longest serving Prime Minister, whose economic reforms shattered the post war consensus. For all these achievements, however, he would be remembered in the public's memory alone for a single speech, given in Birmingham on 20 April 1968.

Powell's 'Rivers of Blood' speech thundered against the impact of immigration from the Commonwealth. Powell referred to a constituent who told him, 'In this country in fifteen or twenty years' time the black man will have the whip hand over the white man.' He spoke of an old-age pensioner who had experienced 'excreta pushed through her letter box' and been stalked by 'wide-grinning piccaninnies'. He lamented, 'Those whom the gods wish to destroy, they first make mad. We must be mad, literally mad, as a nation to be permitting the annual inflow of some 50,000 dependants, who are for the most part the material of the future growth of the immigrant-descended population. It is like watching a nation busily engaged in heaping up its own funeral pyre.'

Powell raged against the Race Relations Bill, which sought to curb racial discrimination, believing it would result in non-white immigrants organising 'to consolidate their members, to agitate and campaign against their fellow citizens, and to overawe and dominate the rest with the legal weapons'. One of Powell's concluding statements foresaw an apocalyptic scenario: 'As I look ahead, I am filled with foreboding; like the Roman, I seem to see "the River Tiber foaming with much blood".'[14] David Feldman tells me, 'For Powell it was race, it wasn't just numbers. The end of Empire and the "world turned upside down" is starkly present in Powell's speech in the most repugnant ways. He talks of the black man holding the whip hand over the white man – an inversion of slavery.'[15]

The very next day, Powell was sacked from his post as Shadow Defence Secretary by Tory Leader of the Opposition, Edward Heath, who was outraged by the tone of Powell's speech as well as some of the claims he had made. As David Feldman rightly points out, it wasn't the impact of Powell's speech itself which drove him into relative obscurity but 'the response of Heath to Powell' by kicking him out of the shadow cabinet.[16] Heath had cast him into the political wilderness for ever, yet Powell had unleashed ugly forces within the nation. His visions of racial conflict appear to have been shared by a large majority of the country. When his arguments were rephrased to state that 'there is a danger of racial violence in Britain unless the inflow of immigrants is cut down by government' and put to respondents in a survey conducted by polling organisation NOP, 78 per cent agreed with the statement.[17]

After the speech Powell received around 120,000 letters, largely from supporters, and it became clear that a majority in the country – confirmed in a Gallup poll as around three-quarters of those questioned – agreed with his speech.[18] Powell strikingly won much working-class support. Over 1,000 east London dockers marched in protest, as did hundreds of meat porters from Smithfield Market in London who were outraged by the demonisation of Powell. 'Enoch Powell was right!' has become a phrase employed by those against immigration ever since. Yet Powell's doomsday scenario, which predicted a national meltdown, even a race war, due to the immigration of non-whites, has never materialised. Enoch Powell was most definitely wrong.

Powell's speech, nevertheless, has certainly had a polarising impact on immigration politics since. It is frequently claimed that the ugliness of the speech meant that immigration was not open for debate for fear of stoking racial tension, which meant people's legitimate and reasonable concerns about the subject went unheeded. In 2013, Nigel Farage – who has described Powell as one of his political heroes – typified this view, claiming that his 'Rivers of Blood' speech was a 'disaster' because it meant 'everybody ran scared of discussing this [immigration] for decades'. His own party, according to Farage, had overturned that legacy by helping to make immigration a 'sensible, moderate, realistic, mainstream debate'. Yet many of the themes of Powell's speech, particularly its hyperbole, can be found in Farage's own immigration rhetoric. Farage's call to scrap racial discrimination laws, as Powell did in his speech, demonstrate that for all his 'moderation' he is in fact not unduly concerned by the existence of racial prejudice.[19]

Whilst radical criticism of immigration may have become something of a taboo, an issue rarely raised by mainstream politicians after Powell's speech, it certainly inflamed the passions of the Tory Party's base. After Powell's speech it became increasingly clear that immigration was becoming one of the central issues for the Conservative Party at a local level. A private survey conducted by the Conservative Political Centre in December 1968 was designed to gather the views of 412 constituency groups. A massive 327 desired immigration to be indefinitely halted and 382 sought strict limitations on the entry of the dependents of those already in Britain, in addition to a five-year embargo on further immigration. Other suggestions put forward by constituency groups included an apartheid-style housing system, even camps to which immigrants could be moved.[20]

Ted Heath, for all his sanctimony after Powell's speech, imposed the strictest immigration controls in British history just three years later. Heath was responding to yet more increased public concern over immigration, unsated by the 1968 Act. In 1972, around two-thirds of the country already believed that it constituted a 'serious social problem'. In the first half of 1976, this had risen to over seven out of ten.[21] The 1971 Immigration Act sought to effectively end primary immigration from the Commonwealth. Employment vouchers were replaced with work permits, which allowed residence on a temporary basis only. It also introduced the notion of 'partiality', which discriminated in favour of immigrants from Australia, Canada and New Zealand over the rest of the (largely non-white) Commonwealth. The Act also introduced some government provisions to assist with voluntary repatriation – although they were not considered stringent enough by Enoch Powell and his ilk.

Heath's policy largely failed to achieve its intended purpose, and immigration in the 1970s continued at around 200,000 per year, much of it from South Asia. This was largely driven by family reunification, which the 1971 Act did not address fully. Despite the imposition of stricter immigration controls, Heath would not be seen as a champion of the substantial and growing anti-immigration voice. Rather, he would soon draw its ire. His government's admission on humanitarian grounds of 27,000 Asians expelled from Uganda by the dictator Idi Amin generated a huge backlash from which anti-immigration extremists gained significant benefit.

The public's perception that successive governments had failed to control the numbers of people entering the country continued to exacerbate concerns. Immigration control was seen as desirable by 66 per cent of those surveyed by NOP in 1978

– double the number (33 per cent) who believed the government should focus on improving race relations. Far fewer approved of the legislation which sought to prevent discrimination against immigrants in employment, housing and society, than supported legislation to restrict the numbers of immigrants coming into the country. Nearly half of the population did not believe there should be any laws to prevent racial discrimination at all. Anti-discrimination laws were widely perceived as 'favouring' immigrants over the native population through positive discrimination. Despite both Labour and Conservative governments' implementation of immigration controls, many members of the public believed they didn't go far enough. The 1968 Commonwealth Immigrants Act, for example, was supported by nearly everyone polled – 90 per cent – but 63 per cent didn't believe the measures were sufficiently stringent. Approximately 75 per cent believed non-white immigration should be halted altogether, and around 60 per cent believed in some form of repatriation.[22]

Wider developments in the 1960s could have provided an opportune moment for the far right to mount a strong challenge. One was rapid British imperial decline. By the late 1960s, practically all of Britain's imperial possessions in Africa and Asia were independent states. The British government had chosen not to fight a series of colonial wars to cling on to the country's possessions following the disastrous Suez campaign in 1956. In a speech to the South African parliament in 1960, Prime Minister Harold Macmillan tacitly acknowledged the inevitability of the end of Britain's Empire in Africa when he spoke of 'the wind of change blowing through this continent. Whether we like it or not, this growth of political consciousness is a political fact. We must all accept it as a fact.'[23] Whilst the country on the whole was indifferent to Britain's loss of Empire, a sizeable chunk of elites were not. It might have provided an opportunity for the far right to build a base from which it could move forward. The immigration issue, however, would prove to be more potent.

Fascists on the march

The 1960s also saw the development of a small but extreme neo-Nazi culture in Britain, which railed against the alleged Jewish role in flooding the country with non-white migrants. Representing only a small number of people, neo-Nazism has nevertheless without question made its mark on the development of the far right. John Tyndall left the LEL in 1958 to co-found the National Labour Party with former LEL and future National Front and BNP activist John Bean. Colin Jordan, on the other hand, had already founded his own, more openly Nazi organisation – the White Defence League – a year earlier. The two organisations soon merged in 1960, and it became quickly apparent that Tyndall and Jordan were kindred spirits united by an intense admiration for Adolf Hitler. They were kicked out of the relatively moderate NLP after setting up a Nazi-style para-military section called Spearhead.

Tyndall and Jordan founded the National Socialist Movement in 1962, on 20 April – not coincidentally Hitler's birthday. This tiny organisation was extreme and reflected an attempt to rehabilitate the interwar German Nazi party in 1960s Britain. Somewhat farcically, Jordan and Tyndall fell out in 1964 – not over politics, but over a girl. Françoise Dior (herself a neo-Nazi and heiress to the French perfume fortune) had been engaged to Tyndall, but dumped him for the more charismatic Jordan, and the two soon married – in a bizarre Nazi-themed wedding ceremony in which each of them pricked the other's finger and shared their 'Aryan' blood.

As the country, and indeed the government, was becoming more sceptical about immigration, the far right remained marginal to the debate. Fractured into several tiny, insignificant and extremist organisations in the mid-1960s, it was clear to many that in order to have any impact on British politics, they would need to pool their resources. When Labour defeated the Conservatives in the 1966 general election for a second time in under two years, it became apparent to the far right that there was a potential market for disgruntled right-wing Tories who were turned off by the unsuccessful and uncharismatic Ted Heath. After a series of negotiations, led by A.K. Chesterton and John Bean, the National Front was formed in 1967, a merger between the LEL, the British National Party (not the same outfit as the contemporary party) and a section of the anti-immigration and white supremacist Racial Preservation Society. Tyndall – much to his annoyance, having been involved in many of the pre-merger talks – was excluded due to his extreme background as a Nazi. However his exclusion would be short-lived and he quietly joined in late 1967. The National Front would prove to be the most successful and threatening far right organisation since the First World War, and would seek to use the public's widespread fear over immigration to catapult it into power.

The National Front was effectively a coalition between far right extremists and neo-Nazis who did not care much for democracy, and hard right conservatives who were democratic but nevertheless anti-immigration and white supremacist. Its first chairman, A.K. Chesterton, jockeyed between the two factions before resigning, exasperated, in 1970. Tyndall would eventually become chairman in 1972, ousting Chesterton's replacement John O'Brien. The party had undergone a potentially fatal split following Tyndall's assumption of power, but they would be saved by an outpouring of anti-immigrant sentiment from the public following Prime Minister Heath's admission of Ugandan Asian refugees. The potential impact of the measure was not lost on *The Times*, who reported that 'the resettlement of Ugandan Asians will provide one of the most severe tests yet of British race relations. It will not be a test willingly undergone.'[24]

This was an opportune moment for Tyndall, and National Front membership soared to approximately 17,500 by the summer of 1973. The timing of Heath's admittance of the refugees was hugely fortunate for a party bitterly divided between extremist and 'moderate', populist factions. As Martin Walker, journalist and author of *The National Front*, notes, 'the single issue which allowed the National Front to climb out of those troubles was the revival of the anti-immigration passions in all their raw fury. General Idi Amin became the saviour of the National Front when he expelled the Ugandan Asians. He was the best recruiting officer the National Front ever had'.[25]

The National Front's performance in local elections began to improve dramatically and by January 1974, the party had thirty branches and fifty-four groups across the country, with particularly strong representation in the south-east and Greater London. Yet this did not translate into electoral success in the early general election called by Ted Heath in 1974. Whilst the party's performance improved again at the year's second general election in October, it still only reflected a minor triumph.

Tyndall was replaced as leader by the more 'moderate' John Kingsley Read following a challenge by the populist wing. An example of the 'moderation' represented by Kingsley Read and the populist faction comes from a speech in 1975 in which he said, 'I am told I cannot refer to coloured immigrants so you will forgive me if I refer to "niggers", "wogs" and "coons".'[26] Kingsley Read also observed, after the murder of Asian youth Gurdip Singh Chaggar in London, 'Last week in Southall, one nigger stabbed another nigger. Very unfortunate. That's one down, one million to go.' He was put on trial for incitement to racial hatred, but cleared. Despite his expulsion, the determined Tyndall returned and resumed his previous role as chairman in 1976 – with Kingsley Read and the populist faction splitting from the party.

The National Front now sought to mount a serious challenge at the Greater London Council elections, according to *The Spectator*, on a 'straight racist platform' and a policy of compulsory repatriation. People 'who are not of Anglo-Saxon stock', according to Martin Webster, would be sent back 'to [their] land of ethnic origin'. For Webster and the National Front, 'A cat born in a kipper box doesn't make the cat a kipper'.[27] They polled a substantial 120,000 votes in the 1977 GLC elections. It appeared perfectly possible that the National Front could pose a threat to mainstream political forces.

Despite this opportunity, Tyndall (and his lieutenant Webster) proved utterly incapable of shedding their extremist, neo-Nazi image; photos of Tyndall parading around in a Nazi uniform during the 1960s did not help, nor did an article written by Webster in 1962 entitled 'Why I am a Nazi', which was re-circulated.

Tyndall's speech at the National Front's Annual General Meeting in 1977, whilst probably not heard by many outside close party ranks, was indicative of his latent extremism. He bellowed, in a manner highly derivative of Adolf Hitler's apoplectic oratory style, 'No power on earth is now going to stop this movement that we have created. No power on earth. No threats. No lies. No words. No laws are going to stop us!' The absurd grandiosity of Tyndall's rhetoric is chilling and amusing to watch in equal measure. A further example of Tyndall's delusions of grandeur was elucidated by John Kingsley Read after he was ousted by Tyndall as leader. Kingsley Read claimed that Tyndall's aims were deeply sinister:

> John Tyndall has told me, and you must understand that I got to know him very well, that his plans are to use the immigrant issue to gain power and then to get rid of the race he hates the most, the Jews. The democratic principle they now pretend to follow is simply a façade. If the Front ever got into power they would never let it go, they would take over the country. Tyndall's wildest dream is to flatten part of the centre of London and make it one big parade ground with government offices all round the edge. He would have 2,000 troops permanently marching around it, so no matter what government building he was in, he could come out onto the balcony and take the salute. All this is well hidden from the bulk of Front members, Tyndall has realised wearing Nazi uniforms is not politically wise. They are now saying that all these early activities were the indiscretion of youth, and that has all changed. But believe me, it is still all there.[28]

Tyndall barely even bothered to disguise his pro-Nazi leanings. In an interview with *The Times*, he described himself as an 'unashamed white supremacist'. His description of his ideal society was almost verbatim neo-Nazi propaganda:

> I would like to see a society in which patriotism and pride of

race were at the forefront and where African, Asian and other
alien cultures were completely rejected. I would like to see
real manhood and real womanhood once again valued, and
the current trend towards unisex reversed. I would like to see
greater emphasis on physical health and fitness, and a much
greater organisation of the young to stop them drifting into
street corners, drugs and degeneration.[29]

Predictions of a National Front ascendency turned out to be
massively overstated. The story of the Front's demise begins in
January 1978, just over a year before the 1979 general election,
when Conservative Party leader Margaret Thatcher addressed
the immigration issue head-on. Asked in a TV interview for
World in Action what she planned to do about immigration, she
immediately cited concern over the growing numbers: 'There
was a committee which looked at it and said that if we went on
as we are then by the end of the century there would be four
million people of the new Commonwealth or Pakistan here.
Now, that is an awful lot.' She went on to say, 'I think it means
that people are really rather afraid that this country might be
rather swamped by people with a different culture.'[30] Thatcher
appeared to have read the public mood effectively – 70 per cent
in a Gallup poll endorsed her 'swamped' remarks.[31]

Thatcher went on to point out, somewhat erroneously, that
'The British character has done so much for democracy, for law
and done so much throughout the world that if there is any
fear that it might be swamped, people are going to react and be
rather hostile to those coming in.' In a manner which characterised postwar attitudes to race and immigration, she argued that
there was something inevitable about the backlash from white
Britons towards immigrants: 'If you want good race relations,

you have got to allay people's fears on numbers.' Clearly, the impact of those numbers was largely negative for Thatcher, who ultimately sought 'an end to immigration'.[32]

The 1979 Conservative manifesto argued similarly that 'firm immigration control for the future is essential if we are to achieve good community relations'. But immigration would decline in importance throughout Thatcher's time in government. She was seen largely as having a firm hand on the tiller. In reality the numbers coming in were minuscule. Indeed, during her first four years of office, there was net emigration from Britain running into tens of thousands. Net inward flows over Thatcher's eleven-year term, although they did increase, were statistically negligible.

At the 1979 general election the National Front polled barely over 1 per cent and descended rapidly into infighting. By running on a platform which pledged to cut immigration further and held out the possibility of 'an end to immigration', Thatcher completely removed from the table the one issue which could have provided them with substantial numbers of votes. Her 'swamped' remarks had already crystallised her as an immigration hawk. Yet we must be cautious in accepting the received wisdom that it was Thatcher who contributed to the decline of the National Front.

As Colin Holmes points out, support for the National Front, rather than demonstrating support for fascism or extreme solutions per se, was 'riding on a wave of pre-existing sentiment' towards immigration. 'Thatcher's emphasis on Britain being "swamped" by immigrants reflected a widely held sentiment rather than merely echoing the claims of the National Front,' Holmes says. 'Do you think Thatcher was worried about the National Front? I wouldn't have thought so, frankly. I think she would have regarded them as insignificant players.'[33] The reality is, such a dysfunctional and extreme organisation simply lacked appeal for the vast majority of the country.

Tyndall was deposed again, this time by his deputy and long-term ally Webster. The party quickly fell into decline and, although it still exists to this day, it has never achieved any form of success since. Following the effective collapse of the National Front in 1979, the far right, despite appearing to have made a breakthrough in the unstable political climate of Britain in the 1970s, was back where it had been two decades before.

By exploring the growth of immigration from the Caribbean and South Asia and the negative public response, we have seen that there was always likely to be demand for anti-immigration politics in Britain. Yet no movement was successful in exploiting the issue. Successive governments since 1962 had been at pains to demonstrate that immigration was under control and had used legislation to achieve this. Those, such as Enoch Powell, who sought to break from this consensus by putting forward more radical solutions were stigmatised by the mainstream. The National Front made an attempt from the fringes to politicise immigration and win support over the issue, but was itself defeated by a combination of stigmatisation, the political manoeuvring of mainstream politicians and, most importantly, the inherent lack of appeal of their extremist ideology.

But Tyndall wasn't done yet. He made another bid for unity and in early 1982, the BNP – consisting of members of a number of minuscule far right parties – was founded.

3
FAR RIGHT MAINSTREAMING, MAINSTREAMING THE FAR RIGHT

'Good morning and welcome to a new edition of ASYLUM! Today's programme features another chance to take part in our exciting competition . . . hijack an airliner to win a council house! We've already given away hundreds of millions of pounds and thousands of dream homes, courtesy of our sponsor, the British taxpayer'. . . 'Iraqi terrorists, Afghan dissidents, pro-Pinochet activists, anti-Pinochet activists, Kosovar drug smugglers, Albanian gangsters, Tamil Tigers, bogus Bosnians, Rwandan mass murderers, Somali guerrillas: COME ON DOWN!'

British National Party, *Identity*,
March–April 2000

Ideologically, upon their founding, the BNP picked up from where the National Front had left off. This meant fanatical British nationalism, the total rejection of 'multiracialism', the repatriation of non-white immigrants, withdrawal from the European Community and a protectionist, economic nationalist agenda. Whilst the BNP would pay lip service to British democratic traditions, they nevertheless maintained a revolutionary neo-fascist position which desired the overthrow of the British constitution and the installation of a new, nationalist state.[1]

However, as Thatcherism ripped through Britain during the 1980s, the far right would experience a long period in the wilderness. Thatcher was unquestionably trusted on issues such as law and order, and – crucially – immigration. The upheavals in the British economy dominated political debate. As long as the Conservative Party was strong on these issues, the far right had little hope of gaining support. It would only be in the late 1990s, with the advent of the New Labour government, that attacks on immigration and multiculturalism would again grow in number and ferocity.

At a European level, it became clear that a party with fascist baggage could be successful. In the 1988 French presidential election, the neo-fascist Front National's Jean-Marie Le Pen received over 4.3 million votes in the first round. The FN and Le Pen had strived to do what Tyndall refused – moderate their image and style in an attempt to gain public respectability. It would take the far right until the twenty-first century to achieve any success and follow a similar path.

The demise of John Tyndall

During the early 1990s, there were, however, rumblings of success for the far right in London's East End. The BNP achieved something of a breakthrough when, in September 1993, following targeted campaigning at the local white population concerned by immigration, Derek Beackon won a seat on Tower Hamlets council. Heralded by Tyndall as the beginning of the BNP's rise, it would in fact be a red herring. The BNP were unable to capitalise on this increase in localised support and Tyndall increasingly resembled a busted flush, with few ideas on how to propel the party into mainstream politics.

Tyndall and the far right were further weakened by a tragedy which occurred in April 1999, bringing the wickedness of far right ideology and violence to public attention. David Copeland, a neo-Nazi who had been a member of the BNP, detonated three nail bombs in Brixton, Brick Lane and outside a gay pub in Soho – targeting the black community, Asians and homosexuals. Three people died, including a pregnant woman, and 140 were injured. Copeland was motivated by the desire to instigate a 'race war' by provoking a backlash from ethnic minorities, subsequently encouraging white Britons to vote for the BNP.[2]

Copeland was given six concurrent life sentences in 2000, and whilst five psychologists diagnosed him with paranoid schizophrenia, his consequent plea of guilty to manslaughter due to diminished responsibility was rejected. Copeland's actions demonstrated the reality of the vicious, conspiratorial ideology of the extreme right – it inevitably leads to violence. Matthew Feldman is an expert on far right terrorism and has testified at court cases against suspected terrorists. Far right terrorists, he argues, 'see themselves as the vanguard, as the Nietzschean superman. They say "I can be the one to tip off the civil war".' A common theme among the most violent right-wing extremists is the idea of 'setting off the race war'.[3] Although Tyndall would not endorse such methods, the reality is that he and Copeland shared a broad ideological platform and differed only over tactics in terms of how to achieve their diabolical aims.

Tyndall's political career in the late 1990s was an unmitigated failure. The public had never turned to the extreme solutions offered by his National Front or the BNP. The main reason is that the environment for fascist organisations throughout had been inhospitable. Interwar fascists had to answer for the excesses of

Hitler and Mussolini, while the spectre of the Holocaust and the Second World War stalked the postwar decades. Tyndall failed to adapt to this postwar environment and barely attempted to conceal his own extremist views, believing that to dilute his political programme would be to sell out. Tyndall would die in 2005 of a sudden heart attack. He probably imagined his death would be slightly more glorious; instead he was found by his wife in his modest home in Hove, West Sussex. The *Guardian* obituary nevertheless described him as a 'racist, violent neo-Nazi until the end'.[4]

Tyndall in many ways personified the far right of the twentieth century. An extremist to his very core, whilst he occasionally cloaked his sinister aims in more typical British patriotism, his worldview was a significant turn-off for the vast majority of Britons, and he was unable to turn anti-immigration sentiment into votes for the far right. In fact, Tyndall was less interested in immigration than he was in traditional fascist ideology, commenting in January 1969: 'Nothing is more depressing than meeting, as one often does these days, people whose political outlook starts and finishes with an embittered sourness towards immigrants. No serious movement in politics can ever function on a sentiment such as this.'[5] In short, he was simply uninterested in breaking into mainstream politics. The aim of his successor, however, was to do just that.

Nick Griffin's fascist makeover

Tyndall's political death had occurred in the summer of 1999 when he was deposed as leader of the BNP by forty-year-old Nick Griffin. Indeed, the story of the BNP's rise begins with the election of Griffin. Under Griffin, the BNP embarked on a new strategy which sought to moderate their appearance, language and style in an attempt to be seen as a legitimate political outfit rather than a clandestine threat to democracy.

Griffin was himself a stalwart of the far right, having started out in the National Front as a teenager. Despite his desire to turn the BNP into a 'respectable' and 'mainstream' party, he was hardly the best man for the job. He was a renowned Holocaust denier who had subscribed to the extreme 'political soldier' faction of the NF. Furthermore, Griffin had, throughout his political life, sought to adapt his political outlook to the current far right zeitgeist, drawing suspicion from experienced members that he was a careerist. To put it mildly, his ideology had a malleability which seemed to acclimatise itself to whatever the situation required.

Griffin sought to transform the BNP into a more populist, campaigning organisation which was 'family friendly' and in tune with local issues. By softening the party's image, he sought to reach out to disenfranchised working-class communities as well as 'middle England'. In its own words, the BNP had 'broadened and deepened its political platform, so that today instead of concentrating on a few, mainly negative issues, it can offer the British people a spectrum of policies ranging across all areas of national life – a policy spectrum which combines to offer a radical populist alternative to the decaying social order around us'.[6]

Rather than obscure neo-fascist theories, compulsory repatriation of non-white immigrants and street demonstrations, the new BNP would seek to be defined by 'freedom', 'democracy', 'security' and 'identity'. As for how it would deal with the age-old accusation of racism, it would now take the initiative and present itself and ordinary white Britons as the victims of 'anti-white racism'. The accusation of fascism would merely be projected onto its opponents: it was violent anti-fascists who were the real fascists. The BNP adopted the style of tabloid jingoism with a working-class face, fulminating against the 'politically correct establishment' who sneered at ordinary working people. They claimed that the three major political parties were all the same – pro-immigration, multiculturalist, spouting endless platitudes about 'diversity' and condemning anyone who disagreed as racist and ignorant.

The party also recognised that many traditional Labour voters were drifting away from the party following Tony Blair's revamp in the 1990s and much of their image change was designed to portray themselves as part of the patriotic working-class tradition – the antithesis of Blair and his clique of diversity obsessives. Labour had abandoned the working man, according to the BNP, and they promoted themselves in staunch Labour-supporting areas in northern England, the West Midlands and east London. One leaflet stated 'BNP is the Labour Party your Grandad voted for', a claim accompanied with a photograph of a miner fresh out of the pit covered in coal dust. They particularly sought to hammer the Labour Party over immigration, with the leaflet stating that 'they brought mass immigration to Britain and flooded the country with cheap migrant labour to undercut British workers'.

Whilst immigration and multiculturalism would be the main issues the BNP used to target voters, in the traditional fascist sense they sought to paint a picture of Britain as a culturally and politically decadent, corrupt mess. One BNP activist, writing for their in-house magazine, *Identity*, was spurred on not by the teachings of Mussolini or Hitler, but by Russell Crowe and Ridley Scott's Roman epic *Gladiator* – which highlighted just how far Britain had fallen: 'In a world of Coca-Cola materialism, gay rights and political corruption and cowardice – "long live" films like Gladiator which inspire people to look towards a better world where decency and honour triumph over greed and selfishness.'[7] Such talk is indicative of the BNP's attempts to ingratiate themselves within mainstream popular culture, so as to seem less alien and appeal to a broader number of voters outside their usual target audience of thugs, criminals and cranks.

One could be forgiven for thinking that the far right genuinely had changed and finally shed its fascist and neo-Nazi baggage. In TV appearances, Griffin sought to sanitise BNP policies in the language of 'common sense'. However, his transformation of the far right reflected not so much a facelift as a mask, which obscured a decades-old fascist grimace. Griffin himself stated in the party magazine *Patriot* that whilst they must speak a new language to the electorate, 'of course, we must teach the truth to the hardcore'.[8] The party's violently racist core ideology, which sought Britain's return to being a homogenously white nation through the removal of non-whites and belief in a global Jewish conspiracy, would only be discussed behind closed doors. Make no mistake, fascism and Nazism were always lurking at the heart of the BNP. Griffin acknowledged that the party's origins lay in the 'sub-Mosleyite wackiness of Arnold Leese's Imperial Fascist League and the Big Government Mania of the 1930s'.[9] Indeed, it appeared that many BNP activists' politics were rooted in the decade where Adolf Hitler seized power in Germany. Shortly before the 2010 general election, short biographies were published of several BNP candidates by the anti-fascist magazine *Searchlight*. They included Barry Bennet, prospective parliamentary candidate for Gosport, who wrote on white supremacist online forum

Stormfront, 'I believe in National Socialism, WW2 style, it was best, no other power had anything like it.'

And whilst he had the ideas to transform the party into a respectable organisation, Griffin's own character made him a somewhat unlikely leader who would always have limited appeal. Many successful far right parties in Europe have relied on a populist and charismatic leader who can directly connect with potential voters. The swashbuckling head of the Austrian Freedom Party, Jörg Haider, for example, who took his party into a coalition government, cut a dashing and charming fig-ure. Griffin on the other hand was no looker, something not helped by his loss of an eye following a bonfire accident in the early 1990s, and certainly not by his considerable gut. He often appeared uncomfortable in his own skin and sought to affect a more affable 'Briddish' accent. Griffin lacked the demagoguery of John Tyndall but was incapable of giving inspiring speeches. One can only speculate as to what the BNP could have achieved with a leader more in the mould of a Haider or Nigel Farage, or indeed anyone who lacked the untrustworthy impression Griffin radiated in media appearances.

Scrounging asylum seekers

Crucially, however, the climate in Britain had become more hos-pitable to the far right message, in part due to an increasingly sensationalist press. Britain has a rich history of right-wing media domination. Prior to the Second World War, the country had a hugely partisan press. Media Baron Viscount Northcliffe owned the *Daily Mail* and *Daily Mirror*, and was succeeded by his brother Viscount Rothermere. Both wielded immense political power. The latter was fiercely anti-left wing, heaped praise on Adolf Hitler and had lobbied strongly in favour of appeasing the Nazi regime in the 1930s. Lord Beaverbrook, another press baron who built the *Daily Express* into Britain's largest newspaper, whilst more moderate than Rothermere, nevertheless had huge influence in British political life and served in numerous cabinet positions as well as Lord Privy Seal during the Second World War.

Following the Second World War, the influence of press barons began to decline in an age where a left-wing economic and social consensus dominated British politics. Editors and newspaper owners had nothing like the power of their interwar predecessors and the public generally valued other sources of political information – such as television, and the opinions of friends, family and colleagues in the workplace – over the print media. Newspapers remained heavily partisan, however: the *Telegraph*, the *Daily Mail*, the *Daily Express* and *The Times* have, since the Second World War, supported the Conservative Party at nearly every general election. *The Sun* had traditionally been a Labour newspaper. After being bought by Rupert Murdoch in 1969, it moved towards the Conservatives in the 1970s and would become one of Margaret Thatcher's staunchest media supporters.

Murdoch had relaunched *The Sun* as a tabloid newspaper almost as soon as he took over. Stories became ever more compact and sensationalised. A (still-running) topless model feature on page 3 was introduced in 1970. After plumping for Thatcher in 1979, it would be the war in the Falklands which would crystallise the reputation of *The Sun* we know today, as assistant editor at the time Roy Greenslade put it: 'xenophobic, bloody-minded, ruthless, often reckless, black-humoured and ultimately triumphalist'.[10] After becoming Britain's highest-circulation newspaper in the 1980s, *The Sun* set the standard for the sensationalised, populist, hyper-nationalist press we still live with.

Asylum seekers and refugees would begin to feel the wrath of the tabloids as soon as numbers began to increase in the late 1990s. The British press has demonstrated contempt for most forms of immigration, but particularly asylum, since the late 1980s. First and foremost, asylum seekers came to be seen as 'bogus', not really fleeing persecution. One cannot discount the racial element of the contempt for asylum seekers – most were from war-torn countries either in southern Europe, Africa or Asia. The idea of thousands of poor, disease-ridden migrants from the third world arriving on a false pretence became common currency.

Under Tony Blair's premiership, the government introduced no less than six pieces of legislation designed to reduce the number of asylum applicants, particularly seeking to reduce the backlog which had grown since the mid-1990s. Labour's 1997 manifesto indicated a tougher stance on immigration, over which, it was argued, Britain must have 'firm control', but particularly promoted measures to deal with the processing of asylum seekers. The notion of preventing 'bogus' asylum seekers was not explicitly used (in contrast with their 1992 manifesto under Neil Kinnock's leadership); however, Labour pledged to 'crack down' on the 'fraudulent use of birth certificates' and 'ensure swift decisions on whether someone can stay or go'.[11]

The 1990s saw a relatively small but unprecedented rise in the numbers of refugees as a result of conflicts, oppressive governments and humanitarian crises. Civil war in Somalia displaced over a million. Following the brutal wars in former Yugoslavia during the 1990s over four million were uprooted. In 1997, there were around seventeen million refugees and asylum seekers in the world – a figure which does not include those internally displaced, which outnumbered even that.[12] Whilst attempts to create a more efficient, technologically advanced system amounted to little in the way of progress, during the early years of New Labour government there was some advancement in getting to grips with asylum in a humane manner.

The number of asylum applications began to steadily rise in Britain from 1996, when there were just under 30,000 applications. In 1999, the figure had grown to over 71,000, and in 2002, a peak of 84,132 was hit. Labour responded by imposing a series of harsh controls designed to reduce the numbers – measures which did cut asylum applications significantly. Following the crackdown on asylum applications and the appeals system, by 2005, the numbers had been radically reduced to 25,712.[13]

An important factor which undoubtedly influenced New Labour's obsession with clamping down on asylum seekers was the overwhelming hostility to foreigners arriving in Britain which occurred in localised areas, such as Dover, whipped up by the media. The *Dover Express* in 1998 published an editorial on asylum seekers which stated, 'we are left with the backdraft of a nation's human sewage and no cash to wash it down the drain'.[14] Claims of an asylum system 'out of control' and of marauding refugees would be the main form taken by anti-immigrant sentiment during much of New Labour's time in office, the agenda of which often appeared dominated by nationalist tabloids.

One report published by the UN magazine *Refugees* provides a succinct overview of the scale of anti-asylum discourse in the media at the turn of the twenty-first century. Between January 2000 and January 2006, 8,163 articles in *The Sun*, the *Daily Mail*, the *Daily Express* and their Sunday versions mentioned the word asylum seeker. That is, on average, just under four *per day*. Public concern becomes more understandable when one recognises the volume of stories being pumped out.[15] It is also little wonder why, in one study, respondents from the British public questioned on 'immigrants' tended to focus on asylum seekers rather than economic migrants, family or students. When the study was conducted, according to figures from the Office of National Statistics, asylum seekers made up around 4 per cent of all inward migration, yet theirs was the word most commonly associated with immigration. The group least focused upon was students, although these were the largest group of immigrants to Britain.[16]

The Sun launched its 'stop the asylum madness' campaign in 2002, lambasting the government for its failure to clamp down on bogus asylum seekers and encouraging readers to cut out and sign coupons, which were then dumped outside the Home Office. Following claims by the paper's editor, Rebekah Wade, that the campaign had 'touched a nerve in the nation', Roy Greenslade, writing in *The Guardian,* clarified that 'For months, rabble-rousing tabloids have been squeezing every sinew in a bid to foment the mass hysteria which has resulted, surprise, surprise, in the worst kind of xenophobic behaviour.'[17] What was more, although the campaign appeared to be critical of the government, it has been claimed that the Labour government was actually complicit in *The Sun*'s action.

Journalist Peter Oborne has said that he acquired a copy of the 'Downing Street grid' – a timetable detailing likely news coverage of key events in the weeks ahead used by Number 10. The grid had *The Sun*'s campaign written down in advance of its launch, on the exact day in which David Blunkett would 'concede' that the government were struggling to control asylum and be quoted saying 'can't argue with *The Sun* over Asylum'. Oborne states, 'What *The Sun* did, which appeared to *Sun* readers to be a spontaneous attack on government policy on asylum seekers, was actually an orchestrated performance with Downing Street . . . it's all choreographed, and it's quite disturbing I think for British democracy.'[18]

One of the main emphases in tabloid representations of the 'asylum panic' was on the sheer volume of people coming to Britain. Not only did the total number of stories give a thoroughly disproportionate impression of how many people were actually arriving, the rhetoric suggested an influx of biblical proportions and no means of controlling it. The *Daily Mail* headlined in December 2002 with 'Now There's One Asylum Claim Every Six Minutes'.[19] One *Daily Express* article, referring to boat refugees entering Spain, was titled 'Next Stop Britain for Boat Refugees'. Shadow Immigration Secretary Damian Green was quoted in the article, disingenuously claiming that 'our borders are more or less completely open'.[20]

Another *Express* article which wrongly conflated illegal immigration and asylum, entitled 'Asylum Seekers: You Can All Stay', claimed that the mere suggestion of any kind of amnesty for illegal immigrants 'underscores fears that illegal immigration is spinning out of control, creating an underclass of ethnic workers'.[21] On another occasion, the *Express* spoke of a 'Tide of Refugees Sitting in Wait Across the Channel', many of whom were 'economic migrants whose sole aim' was 'sneaking across the channel'.[22]

In an article referring to the Sangatte migrant camp in Calais, the *Daily Mail* argued that the police were preparing for a 'mass exodus' from the camp. It was placed alongside the 'chilling figures' relating to asylum: 'One in 20 of the population of

London is either seeking asylum or is a refugee'; 'Two million new homes will have to be built in Britain to house immigrants by the year 2020 at a cost of £125 billion'; 'Asylum seeker support groups have pocketed £58 million in lottery grants from the Community Fund' and finally 'Almost 2,000 people diagnosed in Britain last year with HIV/Aids caught the disease in Africa. It is believed the vast majority were immigrants or asylum seekers infected before arriving in the UK.'[23]

Such hysteria over the volume of asylum seekers clearly had an impact on public perceptions, which consistently and dramatically overestimated the numbers of immigrants and asylum seekers in the UK. In a 2002 MORI Social Research Institute survey, respondents believed, on average, that the UK hosted 23 per cent of the world's asylum seekers and refugees. The accurate figure was 1.98 per cent. Young people were particularly ill-informed about the numbers, believing 31 per cent of the world's asylum seekers and refugees were located in Britain alone.[24] This followed a wider pattern whereby Britons regularly overestimated the number of immigrants in the UK and the nature of ethnic diversity. In a survey conducted by MORI for *Reader's Digest* in 2000, respondents believed that 20 per cent of people in Britain were immigrants, whereas the actual number was 4 per cent. The survey also found that 26 per cent of the country were believed to be of an ethnic minority – the real number was 7 per cent.[25]

The claim that asylum seekers and immigrants brought foreign diseases with them is an old one. Some of the most lurid headlines claimed that they were bringing with them all manner of tropical illnesses, but in particular, HIV and Aids. The *Star* headlined that '1 in 20 Asylum Seekers is HIV [sic]' and that 'treating them stops 12 hospitals from being built'.[26] The

Telegraph reported that 'Aids-infected asylum seekers "overwhelm UK hospitals"'.[27]

The *Daily Express* similarly ran with 'Asylum Seekers spreading Aids around Britain', providing very little evidence in the process. It was argued that 'More than 100,000 asylum seekers – mainly from regions with Aids epidemics – have so far been dispersed from London and the South East to other locations since April 2000 when the scheme was introduced.'[28] A Department of Health official was quoted in the same article rubbishing the story. What was worse, it was claimed asylum seekers were *purposely* spreading the disease. In one undoubtedly tragic case where a female had been infected with HIV by an asylum seeker, the *Daily Star* spoke of 'Evil Sex Assassins' who had committed 'Biological GBH'.[29]

Much like other negative claims surrounding asylum seekers and refugees vigorously promoted in the media, the association with illness and contagious disease was a false flag. There was very little evidence that asylum seekers brought disease with them. In fact, when a screening pilot for tuberculosis was rolled out in Dover, testing around 5,000 asylum seekers over half a year, doctors found plenty of evidence of torture and maltreatment experienced in their country of origin, but not one single case of tuberculosis. A report by the British Medical Association published in 2002 stated that, contrary to media portrayals, asylum seekers were more likely to contract illness after they had come to Britain rather than arrive with pre-existing medical conditions, due to the squalid conditions in which they were forced to live, and a lack of money for maintaining basic health standards.[30]

When disease-ridden asylum seekers weren't being depicted as gathering in their thousands just across the Channel, seeking to live a charmed life at the courtesy of the British taxpayer, perhaps the most common allegation was that they were criminals. They were often wrongly described as 'illegal immigrants', while it was alleged that they tended to be terrorists, violent criminals and thieves.

The *Daily Express* was outraged to discover that the attempted London bombers, whose attack on 21 July 2005 failed after their bombs did not explode, were 'all sponging asylum seekers' who 'raked in more than £40,000 in state benefits . . . Britain gave them refuge and now all they want to do is repay us with death.'[31] There was a deliberate attempt to taint all asylum seekers with the crimes of individuals. The *Sunday People* erroneously stated that 'thousands have already [come to Britain], bringing terror and violence to the streets of many English towns'.[32]

One headline spoke of the 'Asylum Scandal of Baby Killer' who 'should never have been here'. The perpetrator was described as a 'failed asylum seeker' and 'illegal immigrant', while Sir Andrew Green of MigrationWatch was quoted saying that it was a typical 'case of an applicant entirely without merit manipulating the system for years on end. It has become a charade and it is time the system was made much tighter.'[33] The *Star* headlined with 'Kick Out this Scum' after 'failed asylum seeker' Aaron Chisango ran over and killed a twelve-year-old boy whilst drunk and without a driving licence: 'there's only one word for people like Chisango. Scum.' Whilst the article clarified that 'of course, not all asylum seekers are criminals', it nevertheless asserted that 'tragedies like this shame the entire asylum system'.[34]

The fiction that asylum seekers and refugees are more likely to be criminals was disputed by Robert Ayling, Deputy Chief Constable of Kent. Speaking in 2001, he stated that contrary to media portrayals, crime had actually gone down in Dover despite the arrival of asylum seekers: 'As in most groups, the overwhelming majority of asylum seekers are law-abiding citizens. There are criminals who are asylum seekers and often their victims are other asylum seekers.'[35]

One of the principal lines of attack on asylum seekers was about their alleged cosseting and preferential treatment. The *Daily Express* bellowed the headline 'Asylum Seekers Get £20 Million Lottery Money', the article lamenting the fact that this 'huge windfall' (which amounted to around 1 per cent of the total Community fund) for asylum seekers was significantly larger than that spent on indigenous victims of crime and the homeless. Clive Elliot of the Victims of Crime Trust described the 'asylum outrage' as demonstrative of institutionalised racism against the British and called for a boycott of the National Lottery.[36]

The columns of the *Daily Express* were laden with criticisms of charities funding asylum seekers, another article lamenting that 'Diana Fund Pays Out to Gypsies and Asylum Seekers'. The fund, which had already donated money 'to a range of controversial groups, including lesbians and bisexual women in Northern Ireland', was slammed for giving money towards legal support for the children of 'illegal immigrants' and 'a theatre course for asylum seekers'.[37]

The *Daily Mail* similarly criticised the '£100,000 Cost of Choosy Asylum Family', documenting how 'taxpayers have been left with a £100,000 bill after an asylum family claimed damages against a council because they did not like the home they were given'.[38] Schools were similarly shown to be rolling out the red carpet for asylum seekers and other foreigners. This time the *Mail* bemoaned 'The School Where the Pupils have 22 languages', which was blamed on 'an influx of asylum seekers'.[39] Why was Britain allowing all this? Because it was a 'soft touch'.

The public tended to agree. In the same *Reader's Digest* poll cited earlier, a whopping 80 per cent said that the main reason that refugees came to Britain was because the country was a soft touch, with 50 per cent 'strongly' agreeing. Yet there is ample evidence that the public didn't have much idea of what migrants actually received when they arrived as refugees or asylum seekers. The same survey demonstrated that respondents, on average, believed asylum seekers received £113 per week in handouts. The reality was that they got £36.54 per week, which was given to them in vouchers for specific shops and of which only £10 could be converted into cash.[40] And the reality was that asylum seekers had tended to escape poverty in their home countries but continued to live in poverty once they arrived in Britain, rather than living the charmed life the papers sought to portray.

The Sun argued in 2001, 'We resent the scroungers, beggars and crooks who are prepared to cross every country in Europe to reach our generous benefits system.[41] When the *Daily Star* asked its readers to vent their anger after revealing 'how the Government is spending a fortune housing refugees in two swanky hotels', a businessman from Essex said 'it is just rubbing the noses of UK workers in the dirt'.[42] The *Daily Mail* ran with the headline 'Asylum: Yes, Britain is a Soft Touch', arguing that 'The ease with which illegal immigrants could obtain health and education services – and take jobs – helped make the country a magnet.'[43]

A similar article went with 'How "Soft Touch" Britain Tops the Asylum League', stating that Britain had failed 'to crack down hard enough'.[44] Quotes were even provided from asylum seekers to prove the *Mail*'s argument – 'the police threw us in jail. In Italy they swore at us. But once in England, they were extremely nice.' Thus, 'Britain's reputation as a soft touch for asylum seekers was starkly confirmed . . . – by asylum seekers themselves.'[45] The *Daily Star* shouted, 'Asylum: We're Too Damn Soft!', insisting that Britain was 'the asylum capital of the world'.

The 'soft touch' myth is just that – a myth – supported by nothing other than thin anecdotal evidence, as a Home Office report entitled 'Understanding the decision-making of asylum seekers' had already discovered in 2002. The report was specifically commissioned in an attempt to understand the increases in migration, as well as to address 'changes in public opinion towards the issue, as reflected and forged by media representations'. It concluded that there was precious little evidence that asylum seekers had any detailed knowledge of the UK asylum and immigration system or the UK benefits system, and certainly not its comparative favourability to other European countries. Asylum seekers wished to work, rather than being dependent on state benefits. They were primarily attracted by having friends or family based here, by the conviction that the UK was safe, democratic and tolerant, by previous connections to the UK (such as the Commonwealth) and by an ability to speak or learn English.[46] The 'pull-factors' for asylum seekers varied but had very little to do with Britain being a 'soft touch'.

Nick Griffin, writing in January 2000 for the BNP's magazine *Identity*, shortly after he became leader, was nevertheless clearly bullish about the BNP's chances in this new anti-immigrant climate:

Judging from the rash of front-page headlines on the issue, the popular press is clearly finding that shock stories about 'Soft-Touch Britain' strike a chord and sell papers. This in turn will inevitably create a demand for the political expression of anti-immigration feeling, something which no other party is able to provide. Such is the fear of the 'anti-racist lobby' and the ideological liberalisation of the Conservative party that the Tories are unlikely to repeat Margaret Thatcher's race card trick; the media are setting up goals for an anti-immigration party to score, and we're the only one in the field.[47]

The consequences of the media's coverage of asylum at the turn of the twenty-first century were significant. It set the agenda for how all forms of immigration would subsequently be viewed, and perpetuated the notion of marauding foreigners in their thousands invading Britain. Alongside this, mainstream politicians, such as the leader of the Conservative Party, were describing Britain as a 'foreign land' – thus legitimising anti-migrant, xenophobic sentiment. The stage was now set for the far right, who themselves were seeking an entry into British politics. We will now turn to the unprecedented rise of those elements of the far right who were propelled by this new climate, further entrenching anti-immigration politics in the national debate.

4

THE RISE AND FALL OF THE BNP

*Our war heroes defied European dictators, riding out the storms
of war to preserve our traditional British Christian values . . . In
World War II the sacrifice of our heroes saved not just Britain from
invasion, but the whole of Europe from the evil Nazi plan to create
a totalitarian European super-state. Our war heroes fought like
lions to stop them being swamped by foreign invaders. What would
the mates they left behind think if they could see Britain today?
What's it coming to when you are made to feel like an unwelcome
foreigner in your own country?*

Nick Griffin,
speaking on BBC *Question Time*, 22 October 2009

Hostility to asylum seekers in the tabloids, and criticism
of New Labour's 'soft' asylum policy corresponded with a
charged debate over British identity as the twenty-first century began. It is somewhat ironic that the rise of the far right
would occur shortly after a new liberal dawn appeared to have
transformed British politics. Tony Blair was elected in 1997
by a landslide and on a wave of public enthusiasm and optimism. The party's general election theme was the peppy pop
song, 'Things can only get better' by D:Ream. As the sun rose
over the Thames the morning after the election, Blair spoke
to throngs of Labour supporters shouting 'Tony! Tony!' before

proudly exclaiming, to ecstatic cheers, 'A new dawn has broken, has it not?'

New Labour sought to equip Britain for the twenty-first century and the challenges of globalisation, a future which held so much promise. Giving a speech on the Millennium Dome, home of a grandiose exhibition in Greenwich to mark the turning of the millennium, Blair told the audience: 'In this experience, I want people to pause and reflect on this moment about the possibilities ahead of us, about the values that guide our society . . . It will be an event to lift our horizons. It will be a catalyst to imagine our futures.'[1] Blair's Britain had promised a new era of tolerance, an acceptance of diversity and multiculturalism. As Blair himself had boldly proclaimed: 'I want a Britain that does not shuffle into the new millennium afraid of the future, but strides into it with confidence.'[2] Britain's new swagger, dubbed a little embarrassingly by commentators 'Cool Britannia', was predicated on an embrace of the country's multiracial character as a strength rather than a challenge to be overcome.

Robin Cook articulated the idea in his 'chicken tikka masala' speech to the Social Market Foundation in April 2001, before that year's general election. Referring to opponents of immigration, the EU and devolution, he stated: 'Sadly, it has become fashionable for some to argue that British identity is under siege, perhaps even in a state of terminal decline.' The Foreign Secretary sought to 'celebrate Britishness' and in particular, its multiculturalism:

Chicken Tikka Masala is now a true British national dish, not only because it is the most popular, but because it is a perfect illustration of the way Britain absorbs and adapts external influences. Chicken Tikka is an Indian dish. The Masala sauce was added to satisfy the desire of British people to have their meat served in gravy. Coming to terms with multiculturalism as a positive force for our economy and society will have significant implications for our understanding of Britishness.[3]

New Labour's embrace of multiculturalism was guided principally by the demographic realities of contemporary Britain, as well as by the rapidly changing, globalised world. It also reflected a challenge to the Conservative Party, which was regularly portrayed as out of touch with modern Britain, particularly in terms of its members' attitude towards ethnic minorities, which ranged from indifference to hostility. Robin Cook's address came a month after Conservative leader William Hague's now somewhat infamous 'Foreign Land' speech to the Spring Forum in Harrogate.

Hague, rather than celebrating diversity, lamented the condition of Britain and grimly envisaged four more years of Labour – 'let me take you to a foreign land', he said. Hague's vision was nothing short of dystopian. He spoke of 'The Royal Mint melting down pound coins as the euro notes start to circulate. Our currency gone forever . . . the Chancellor returning from Brussels carrying instructions to raise taxes still further . . . jail doors opening as thousands of criminals walk out early to offend again.' Hague talked of both an asylum 'crisis' and a 'mess', pledging an end to Britain being a 'soft touch . . . Talk about tax and they call you greedy. Talk about crime and they call you reactionary. Talk about asylum and they call you racist. Talk about your nation and they call you little Englanders. This government thinks Britain would be alright if only we had a different people.'[4]

Hague was criticised by many across the political divide,

including Robin Cook. Liberal Democrat leader Charles Kennedy slammed Hague's use of 'Enoch Powellesque language . . . conjuring up images of a "foreign land" overrun with scrounging immigrants is no way to lead a responsible debate', he argued.[5] The notion of Labour and the political establishment favouring immigrants and asylum seekers over natives, already a tabloid favourite, would become a palpable feature of British political discourse for years after.

Hague's speech pales in comparison to that of Enoch Powell in 1968 both in terms of the extremism of its content and the ferocity with which it was delivered, and it had a very different impact on the political landscape. The immigration and asylum debate had been nevertheless been opened up and legitimised by the Leader of Her Majesty's Opposition. To use another analogy much beloved by critics of immigration, the floodgates had been opened and a tsunami of anti-immigrant rhetoric was to wash over British political culture.

Extremism thrives

During the BNP's electoral rise, immigration itself in Britain would dramatically increase, as would public concern over it. Griffin's attempt to professionalise the party and ensure they were in tune with local issues bore fruit relatively quickly. The BNP began to pick up a small number of local council seats and generally increase its vote share. In local elections in 2002, it gained three seats in Burnley and polled an average of 16 per cent. The media began to pay closer attention to the BNP as its performance improved. However, the coverage was far from positive for the party, even in right-wing newspapers which frequently railed against immigration and multicultural-ism. Arch-conservative columnist Peter Hitchens, writing in the *Mail on Sunday*, described the BNP as a 'functioning Nazi party' and 'revolting, racist and cruel'.[6] In another column later that year by Hitchens, he was under no illusions that despite Griffin's makeover, the party remained 'fascist'.[7]

The party's fortunes reached unprecedented heights in 2003's local elections, where they held an average vote share of just over 17 per cent and picked up thirteen council seats. Much like the brief pockets of success for the NF in the 1970s, the external climate probably contributed more than the BNP's own activities. Immigration and asylum had become a serious issue in the mainstream press, leading stalwart John Bean to believe that the time was ripe for a BNP upsurge: 'As our once great and wonderful country surrenders to the masses of asy-lum seekers from the less civilised parts of the world, I am convinced that the British National Party really does have tre-mendous potential to become a serious political power.'[8]

Then came 9/11. The 11 September attacks in the United States led to a new stigmatisation of Muslims in Britain and a growth in anti-Muslim attacks. Areas where the BNP began to gain support, such as the Lancashire towns of Oldham and Burnley, had experienced unprecedented racial tension between Asian and white inhabitants – in the case of both leading to all-out rioting, in the spring and summer of 2001 respectively.

Media coverage of the BNP itself however was utterly hostile, despite the intense scrutiny of issues such as immi-gration, multiculturalism and crime. The *Daily Express* ran an explicitly anti-BNP campaign, a columnist stating that 'any reader who actually voted BNP should consider themselves ineligible to buy this newspaper'.[9] Peter Hitchens admitted the paradox which lay at the heart of the BNP during this period of success: 'On the one hand [the BNP] is a cunning and skilful voting machine, on the other ingrained and discredited racial theories, Holocaust deniers, nose measurers and violent oafs.' Whilst Hitchens was impressed at the BNP's ability to tap into local issues after meeting Griffin and local activists, they were nevertheless a 'sinister sect of creeps, misfits and racists'.[10]

The BNP would continue to build on the success of the 2003 local elections. Initially, they were disappointed not to win any seats in the European Parliament a year later, despite gaining around 750,000 votes, usurped by TV personality Robert Kilroy-Silk's right-wing Ukip. The latter was not the anti-immigration party it would become a few years later. Ukip at this point, whilst to the right of the Conservative Party, was a single-issue party (promoting withdrawal from the EU) which primarily attracted right-wing Tories. Ukip would regularly put in a strong performance at Euro elections, but the BNP tended to outperform it at a local level and was without doubt the most well-known anti-immigration party.

Press coverage remained hostile to the BNP. Following a BBC documentary which broadcast secretly filmed footage of a number of BNP activists, including Griffin, exposing the hard-line racism which ran through the party, *The Sun* ran the headline 'BNP: Bloody Nasty People'. What followed was an article which described the BNP as a 'collection of hate-filled moronic thugs . . . wicked men . . . criminals who should be locked up'.[11] Such unmistakable venom spread by Britain's most popular newspaper did not however dim the prospects of the BNP, who would benefit from the very same paper's relentless and xenophobic criticisms of migration.

The Iron Curtain is raised

While mass hysteria over asylum seekers was to frame Britain's relationship with immigration in the early twenty-first century, it would be economic migration and the accession of eight former Communist countries from East-Central Europe in 2004 which would transform that relationship. Labour had introduced increasingly stringent measures to restrict applications for asylum, but at the same time they championed economic migration, which Home Secretary David Blunkett referred to as 'managed migration'. The problem with this description is that economic migration was now subject to less 'management' than at any point since the early 1960s. The UK government was one of only three EU member states (the others being Sweden and Ireland) not to impose temporary controls on migration from new members, in keeping with their commitment to encourage economic migration as a relief to the economy.

Given that migration within the EU had been generally negligible before 2004, the government predicted that only around 13,000 per year would move to Britain from new EU member states. This was a catastrophically wrong prediction, as between May 2004 and June 2005, over 230,000 had already arrived. In the summer of 2016, the number of workers from 2004 accession countries living in the UK passed one million. Former Home Secretary Jack Straw admitted in 2013 that Labour had made a 'spectacular mistake' in lifting the transitional controls in 2004.[12] This had meant that migrants who might have gone to other prosperous countries in western Europe, such as Germany, France or Italy, tended to favour Britain.

The flow of immigration which followed the accession of

the A8 EU countries, having already begun slightly before, has resulted in the largest influx of migrants in British history. In 2004 net migration stood at 268,000, and it remained at a similar level for the next decade.[13] Whilst eastern European immigration was not a new phenomenon, the scale at which people were settling was unprecedented. Towns, villages and cities previously with tiny foreign-born populations rapidly developed vibrant and expanding communities from Poland, Lithuania and Latvia. Migration from the East was treated by the media in a similar manner to the 'asylum panic' of the late 1990s and early 2000s; but now politicians were only too happy to join in, fanning the flames of public resentment.

The largest influx of EU migrants following the 2004 accessions came from Poland. The fact that, relatively quickly, Poles cemented a reputation for being incredibly hard-working and decent, qualities without which the British economy would struggle, did not stop a barrage of anti-Polish headlines appearing in the *Daily Mail*, which prompted the Polish Federation of Great Britain to report the paper to the Press Complaints Commission, accusing them of stoking 'negative emotions and tensions between the new EU immigrants and local communities'. These stories were typical of the rhetoric over asylum seekers – seeking to portray Poles as an alien 'invasion' of foreigners which was creating nothing but a drain on resources.

Some of the headlines included: 'Britain Is Country of Choice for Many "Feckless" Poles'; 'Polish Borat Claims Groping Women Is Normal in Eastern Europe'; 'Polish Homosexuals Facing Persecution in Exodus to UK'; 'Polish Immigrants Take £1bn out of the UK Economy'; 'Immigrants Here for Good: Half of Poles Plan to Stay in UK'; 'Fears for NHS & Schools as 1,000 Polish Children Are Born Every Month'. Even when trying to defend themselves, the newspaper could not resist creating dramatic analogies: 'The Mail is entitled to run stories about immigration, the more so as the last 10 years have witnessed immigration on a scale at a vastly increased rate than at any time in this country's history since and including the Norman invasion of the 11th century.'[14]

The public, who have consistently since the Second World War advocated restrictions on immigration, responded once more by dramatically increasing demands for curbs.

Attitudes towards the impact of migration became stridently more negative in the first decade of the twenty-first century. In 2002, those who believed immigration had a negative economic impact stood at 43 per cent, whereas those who saw immigration as having a negative cultural impact stood at 33 per cent. In 2011, following high levels of net migration, 51 per cent believed immigration had a negative economic impact, and 48 per cent a culturally negative one. In the same year, the proportion of those advocating a reduction in immigration had risen to 75 per cent from 63 per cent in 1995, with 51 per cent in favour of a 'large reduction'.[15]

Panic over asylum continued. As discussed earlier, the intense and negative tabloid focus on asylum obscured the fact that the vast majority of immigrants were neither asylum seekers nor refugees. Immigration had nevertheless become crystallised in the public mind as being heavily linked with the seeking of asylum.

In 2000, 43 per cent of the public believed asylum seekers and refugees to be economic migrants seeking to enter the country on false pretences to better their standard of living – this contrasts with 1997, where only 11 per cent made such a claim. Ultimately a hyperbolic and fact-free immigration debate had the effect of linking all forms of migration – skilled and non-skilled, EU and non-EU, asylum seekers, refugees and students – within one category. EU migration from eastern Europe was heavily conflated both with asylum and with racial division within Britain, and all the surrounding negativity.

Ironically, the far right has long seen the mainstream media as its enemy. Writing for *Identity*, the dim-witted Paul Golding (now leader of far right party Britain First) said of the media: 'We in the BNP know only too well that the mass media, and the deceitful low-life journalists that infest it, are liars. They lie all the time, every day, every hour, and in every new story.'[16] Yet more perceptive activists recognised that the media had been fuelling demand for anti-immigration politics. One activist writing in *Spearhead* said:

> So much is now published in parts of the mainstream press about multi-culturalism, illegal immigration and 'health tourism' that writers in this journal can take a back seat for a while and let them all get on with it. For once, we don't have to cobble together the odd facts and figures previously released by a nervous and inhibited media; now the floodgates (both the migrants and the journalism about migrants) are open wide, with many writers even apologising for keeping the subject under wraps for so long.[17]

Similarly, prominent BNP spokesman Simon Darby couldn't believe his and the party's luck that 'Newspapers have become obsessed with the asylum issue. I have not been able to believe the *Daily Express*. Issue after issue, day after day, asylum this, asylum that. So we now have the luxury of banging on people's doors with the mainstream issue of the day . . . It has legitimised us. We are mainstream now.'[18] The BNP may have been a throwback to the 1930s, but its rise was very much located in the revolt against asylum seekers and immigrants in the twenty-first century.

Immigration would remain centre-stage during the 2005 general election and was ranked high in polls looking at issues rapidly growing in importance for the electorate. Tony Blair, now entering into his third election as leader, was certainly vulnerable on the issue (as he was on the Iraq war). His opponent, Michael Howard, himself directly descended from Romanian-Jewish immigrants, sought to use immigration as a means to attack a purportedly out-of-touch Labour government. The Conservative Party visibly proclaimed in a billboard campaign that 'it's not racist to impose limits on immigration'.

A speech by Howard in Telford on immigration in April 2005 echoed that of William Hague four years earlier: 'Let's be clear. It's not racist to talk about immigration. It's not racist to criticise the system. It's not racist to want to limit the numbers. It's just plain common sense.' Howard went on to state that 'it is offensive to brand as racist hard working people who worry about the chaos in our immigration system'.[19] He comfortably lost the election, with Blair winning a historic third term – although the continuation in power of a Labour Party already mortally wounded in the mind of the right-wing press over immigration, meant the persistence of anti-immigrant sentiment in the media.

Which the BNP capitalised on. The issues of immigration, and particularly of multiculturalism, were becoming more and more salient in elite discourse among the media and politicians alike. *Spectator* columnist Rod Liddle, himself a critic of immigration and multiculturalism, acknowledged that the concerns of the BNP were being brought into the mainstream by elite commentators and politicians. Speaking of Nick Griffin, he stated:

> A racist he may be – although he takes the time to deny it every so often – but what he actually says scarcely deviates these days from what we might call the New Orthodoxy: Muslims are a bit of a problem and we're letting in far too many immigrants. You will have heard one or another of those sentiments expressed in the last couple of years by Jack Straw, Trevor Phillips, David Cameron, Polly Toynbee and so on.[20]

Dr Aurélien Mondon is a Senior Lecturer at Bath University and an expert on the far right. He told me that mainstreaming is 'not just the BNP becoming more mainstream and changing their strategy, it is also the mainstream changing and accepting things that were not acceptable. You cannot have one without the other.' As we have already seen, 'you can't have the far right mainstreaming itself without the mainstream helping it at the same time'. Mondon used the fallout from 9/11 as an example of how previously unacceptable ideas gained respectability: 'You cannot understand the mainstreaming of racism and anti-immigration politics without looking at the response to 9/11 which legitimised anti-Muslim sentiment. It allowed people to bring back racist ideas to the forefront of politics because it wasn't being against Arabs any more, it was about being against Muslims. So you're not against an ethnicity or a race, but a religion.'[21]

Despite the reality of multiculturalism as a relatively benign phenomenon which largely seeks to manage the complexity of Britain's diverse communities, many prominent right-wing commentators view it as a pernicious cancer in British life and symptomatic of national decline. Melanie Phillips, a right-wing columnist for the *Daily Mail* and *The Times*, in her anti-Islamic polemic *Londonistan: Britain is Creating a Terror State from Within*, has a somewhat apocalyptic and conspiratorial vision of multiculturalism. For her, multicultural policies are less to do with the realities of diverse postwar Britain and more of a plot by the British establishment, enchanted by the 'revolutionary left', who believe that 'Britain in particular, and the nation in general . . . had to be unravelled and a new order constructed from principles untainted by the exclusive particulars of national culture'.[22] Multiculturalism 'has become the driving force of British life, ruthlessly policed by a state-financed army of local and national bureaucrats enforcing a doctrine of state-mandated virtue to promote racial, ethnic and cultural difference and stamp out majority values.'[23]

Since the attacks in London of 7 July 2005, which killed fifty-six people and were committed by four British Muslims, right-wing politicians and commentators have sought to link multiculturalism with terrorism. Phillips makes the tenuous link between multifaith schools in Dewsbury, West Yorkshire, and the leader of the 7 July bombers, Mohammad Sidique Khan. Dewsbury, in which a large Muslim community lives, was the 'home town for a while' of Khan, and consequently, for Phillips, illustrative of 'a trend that has transformed the whole of British life during the past four decades – one which has drastically weakened it from within to the threat from without. That trend is multiculturalism.'[24] Phillips goes on to argue that multiculturalism has 'unwittingly fomented Islamist radicalism in the sacred cause of "diversity"'.[25]

Following a failed attempt in 2007 by Islamist extremists to detonate two car bombs in London, an article in *The Spectator* by Rod Liddle argued that the plot was 'the predictable consequence' of multiculturalism (as well as 'lax immigration, mad human rights laws and neocon aggression'). After casting doubt on the claim by the BBC's 'bizarrely pro-Islamist' reporter Frank Gardner (an unsavoury reference to the fact that Gardner was left paralysed in an ambush by al-Qaeda sympathisers in Saudi Arabia in 2004) that British Muslims were appalled by the attempted attack, Liddle stated, 'We are told these sorts of things in order to stop us coming to unpalatable conclusions, because the government still clings, ever more precariously, to the vestigial tail of that discredited ideology, multiculturalism.'[26]

Liddle's portrayal of an elite obsessed with the virtues of multiculturalism was at odds with reality. Less than six months earlier, Gordon Brown had attacked the phenomenon, stating that 'we are waking from a once-fashionable view of multiculturalism, which, by emphasising the separate and the exclusive, simply pushed communities apart'.[27] There was also a wider sense that the multiculturalism of Robin Cook's 'chicken tikka masala' speech in 2001 was in decline, and was certainly not being relentlessly pursued. The mythical liberal establishment, so often the scourge of right-wing attacks, was in fact notable by its absence in defending multiculturalism – an idea which fewer and fewer were prepared to preserve.

Within this climate, the 2006 local council elections would reflect the far right's greatest triumph and there were growing concerns that the BNP was here to stay. Jon Cruddas, Labour MP for Dagenham, was particularly concerned about BNP success in his own constituency: 'I would not underestimate the strength of what they are tapping into. The alienation. The sense of disenfranchisement, the social immobility and this feeling that the political classes have been completely removed from their day-to-day life experiences . . . the sense, I suppose, that no one is on their side.'[28]

Less than a year after the 7/7 London bombings, the BNP made opposition to Islam a strong campaigning issue. They were rewarded with thirty-three council seats and a national vote share of just over 19 per cent. Their continued rise did not lead to more favourable press coverage, and right-wing tabloids continued to attack the party. A *Daily Mail* article written by Richard Littlejohn stated, 'Fortunately, most people weren't taken in by this bunch of Toytown Nazis. But even one BNP councillor is one too many. It's nauseating to discover that decent people would even consider voting for this loathsome bunch of sociopaths.'[29]

Fellow right-wing columnist Melanie Phillips similarly attacked the BNP in the *Jewish Chronicle* for its attempts to mask anti-Semitism within the party. She described them as 'visceral Jew-haters', attempting to 'bury their reputation for thuggery and neo-fascism, and to pose instead as a respectable nationalist party defending Britain against the threat to its way of life'.[30] In another article for the *Daily Mail*, Phillips described the BNP as a 'rabidly racist and anti-Semitic party . . . its attacks on Islam are a fig-leaf for prejudice against all Muslims, Asians and minorities'.[31]

Despite much common ground over the key issues facing Britain, criticism of the BNP in the mainstream print media before the 2009 European elections, where it was feared the party could win seats in the European Parliament, reached new heights. *Daily Mail* columnist Harry Phibbs was under no illusions about the party's true nature:

The BNP are neo Nazis. They have a National Socialist ideology.

Their founder John Tyndall, who used to pose in Nazi uniform, was on record as saying: 'Mein Kampf is my bible.' His successor and protégé Nick Griffin might be more circumspect but he worked hand in glove with Tyndall for many years. Griffin enjoys cordial relations with David Duke of the Ku Klux Klan and with the openly neo-Nazi German group the National Democratic Party ... Griffin denies the existence of Nazi death camps.[32]

While many of the right-wing tabloids sought to delegitimise the BNP by pointing out their true, extremist nature, one article in the *Daily Telegraph* reflected a different approach – ridicule: 'We British have a far cleverer weapon than outrage to deploy against the BNP, the smart bomb all demagogues fear: laughter ... there is nothing like spending a day with them in their key target county of Essex to see them not as terrifying heavies but as light entertainment. March on Rome? I'm not sure they could march on Romford.' Referencing the controversy surrounding the invitation of BNP London Assembly member Richard Barnbrook and Nick Griffin to a Buckingham Palace garden party, the article went on: 'Griffin may yet munch the Queen's cucumber sarnies, while MPs eat more humble pie. But the BNP are simply too stupid ever to kiss hands and take up the seals of office. It's hard to laugh but they are just a joke.'[33]

The elections, however, came at an unfortunate time for those hoping for stagnation in the BNP's rise, the vote occurring just months after the MPs' expenses scandal. The uncovering of widespread abuse by Members of Parliament and the House of Lords of generous financial expenses cannot be underestimated as an event which crystallised derogatory perceptions of politicians. It contributed to the view that they were 'on the take', with 68 per cent believing that most Members of Parliament 'make a lot of money by using public office improperly'. Following the scandal, a mere 20 per cent polled for Ipsos MORI were satisfied with the way that Parliament did its job, with 71 per cent dissatisfied with the House of Commons. Over three-quarters – 76 per cent – did not trust MPs in general to tell the truth; 68 per cent believed that at least half of Members of Parliament 'use power for their own personal gain', with 40 per cent believing most or all did. Forty-eight per cent believed that at least half of MPs were corrupt.[34]

Both the press and the public were outraged, and the BNP sought to tap into anger directed towards the political establishment. Their campaign literature promised to 'punish the pigs'. The *Daily Mail* saw how this anger could lead to unprecedented success for the far right. Columnist Martin Samuel pleaded with readers to 'spoil a ballot paper, set fire to it for all I care, or use this as an opportunity to find out who is your best candidate that can be corralled on party lines; but do not vote for the BNP. It isn't big, it isn't clever and it certainly isn't any way to protest. You want to change politics, then stop hiding behind the skirts and suits of a bunch of fascists.'[35] Under the headline 'The Truly Nasty Party', a comment article read more apocalyptically: 'The Mail fully shares voters' dismay over the Commons expenses scandal and the mainstream parties' failure to tackle such issues as unrestricted immigration. But if they are driven into the arms of the BNP, they'll turn a crisis into an appalling tragedy – and betray the millions who've died to keep Britain free.'[36]

Yet the BNP continued to rise, reaching the apex of their success in 2009 when they stunned the country by winning two seats in the June elections for the European Parliament. They had continued to rail against the government for 'mass immigration' and had previously used opposition to predominantly European immigration from the EU as a chance to shed their racist image: 'The BNP opposes immigration into the UK from whatever its source. For forty years this immigration has primarily been coloured. But it is not an issue of colour since the party is equally opposed to immigration from Albania and Eastern Europe.'[37] Labour finished in third place in the election – behind Ukip, who secured just under 2.5 million votes. The BNP received just under 1 million. The electoral map was shifting, and it was going rightwards, predominantly over the issue of immigration.

Whilst the BNP remained a relatively minor feature of the political landscape, Nick Griffin had taken the far right to unprecedented heights. Following the party's strong performance, the *Daily Mail* lamented its election success. Columnist Paul Harris, observing Griffin in Manchester Town Hall as it was becoming clear he was about to win a seat, said he 'had the kind of smile that bullies wear when they know they think they've got away with it'. Nevertheless, Harris welcomed the increased scrutiny the party would receive following the election of a member to the European Parliament. Referencing Griffin's claim that the party was non-racist, he observed, 'That's going to be a very difficult stance for the BNP to maintain over the next five years in Europe.'[38] Peter Oborne was more alarmist, describing Griffin as 'by far the most successful leader of the far right Britain has ever produced . . . The BNP is a terrifying new force in British politics, and this is a very scary moment in our national history.'[39]

Digging their own fascist grave

The night of 22 October 2009 could have been the making of the BNP and taken them fully into the mainstream. Following the party's success at the European Parliament elections four months earlier, the BBC invited Nick Griffin to be a panellist on their flagship politics broadcast *Question Time*. It was a highly controversial move, sparking numerous complaints from politicians and protests from anti-fascist groups. Here was Griffin, a racial nationalist and neo-fascist who had openly questioned the Holocaust, being provided a platform on which he would be watched by millions of people nationwide.

Despite appearing slightly shifty, particularly when he was asked about his conviction for incitement to racial hatred following comments written about the Holocaust in the 1990s, Griffin sought to present the BNP as a patriotic and above all, legitimate party, standing against immigration and multiculturalism. Audaciously, he invoked the memory of Winston Churchill (in the same way the BNP did on much of their party literature), arguing that the country's greatest hero would be appalled at the state of modern Britain, tapping into a very British sense of patriotism rather than the violent fanaticism or Hitler-worship of the past.

The initial reaction of the print media was of ridicule and derision at Griffin's performance. Max Hastings, writing for the *Daily Mail*, described Griffin as 'a pudgy middle-aged racist who doubts whether Hitler killed six million Jews . . . The panel had little difficulty making Griffin seem slippery and indeed repugnant'. By providing a platform to Griffin, 'it showed what an empty vessel he is'.[40] Amanda Platell, in similarly unflattering terms, described Griffin as 'the ogre at the panto', while Stephen Robinson argued that Griffin had wasted his opportunity: 'a cleverer fascist would have exploited that unprecedented platform to become a major national political figure'.[41] The *Mail* nevertheless took issue with the hectoring of Griffin by the audience and panellists throughout the episode: 'What's so disappointing about *Question Time* was the crass, cack-handed way the show subjected Mr Griffin to little better than a cross between a public lynching and a show trial.'[42]

Question Time ultimately proved neither the making nor the breaking of the BNP. Initial responses seemed to imply that Griffin's appearance had led to an immediate increase in support for the party and a vindication of those advocating 'no platform'. A YouGov poll taken shortly after the broadcast found that 22 per cent of voters were 'seriously' considering voting for the BNP at a future election. And whilst support for the party itself was shown to be limited, some 43 per cent said that they shared some of the BNP's concerns, while 12 per cent agreed entirely.[43]

There was much promise for the BNP as the 2010 general election loomed. Although immigration would not be a prominent issue in the 2010 campaign, being a subject which all three major parties generally sought to avoid, perhaps one of the most significant moments concerned east European migration – so-called 'Bigotgate'. When on a walkabout in Rochdale, Prime Minister Gordon Brown was confronted by Gillian Duffy, a 65-year-old council worker and Labour voter. Animated, Duffy remarked, 'You can't say anything about the immigrants. All these eastern Europeans what are coming in – where are they flocking from?' Brown responded politely, without answering her question, before entering a car, a microphone still on his lapel. The grouchy Prime Minister was then heard dismissively calling Duffy 'a sort of bigoted woman' who 'said she used to be Labour'.[44] In a few seconds, Brown had appeared to confirm the worst suspicions of millions of British voters – that when the cameras were off, British politicians were dismissive of ordinary Britons' concerns over immigration. It was exactly the kind of slip-up that could have caused an entry point for the BNP.

Nevertheless, Griffin and the BNP were unable to turn either their brief period in the limelight or Brown's gaffe into more electoral success. They polled just under 2 per cent nationally – albeit achieving a not insubstantial 560,000 votes – but never came close to winning a seat. Even in Barking, where Griffin had sought to depose long-standing Labour MP Margaret Hodge, he could only achieve third place and 14.8 per cent of the vote. The 2010 election marked the beginning of the end for Griffin and the BNP and they saw a rapid decline in support, losing many of their elected councillors.

True to far right form, the party descended into infighting after the election. The party's other MEP, former neo-Nazi Andrew Brons, sought to oust Griffin as leader but Griffin narrowly won the subsequent leadership election. Brons left to form his own party, cutting the BNP's representation in the European Parliament in half. It also soon became clear that the party's finances were in disarray. Griffin was declared personally bankrupt in early 2014, shortly before losing his seat in the European Parliament in May. By the 2015 general election, Griffin had been expelled from the party and they fielded a pitiful eight candidates nationwide. The BNP was at this point – as it remains, to all intents and purposes – finished.

The BNP's collapse should not only be seen as a failure, but as a return to form for the far right. Over the past 100 years, as we have seen, the far right has largely existed as a fringe movement, barely scratching the surface of electoral success. It has more often than not been seen as alien, extreme and downright weird. However, to assess the impact of the far right by conventional means – in terms of elections and formal political power – is to misread its impact and ideas. Despite the moral panic surrounding the rise of the BNP, the truth remains that electoral politics has always been an area of little success for the far right. The impact of their activity lies elsewhere.

Following the BNP's collapse, anti-immigration and Islamo-phobic politics turned from the ballot box to the street. 2009 saw the emergence of a new, anti-Muslim, street-based move-ment – the English Defence League. The EDL was not a formal political party interested in competing at elections, but was instead concerned with wreaking havoc in English towns and cities. Between 2009 and 2013, it organised hundreds of follow-ers to march through the streets (most often those with large Muslim populations) in defiance of 'radical Islam'. Given that a significant proportion of the EDL's support was recruited from football hooligan groups, violence inevitably ensued at these marches between EDL activists, the local community and the police, as well as anti-fascist counter-demonstrators.

In originating from other small anti-Muslim movements and football hooligan subculture, rather than from any political organisation, the EDL marked a break with the traditional far right. Nigel Copsey, Professor of History at Teesside University and Co-Director of the Centre for Fascist, Anti-Fascist and Post-Fascist Studies, has argued that the EDL is 'best understood as an Islamophobic, new social movement, born of a particularly unattractive and intolerant strand of English nationalism'.[45] It professed to be anti-racist, multiracial, and pro-gay rights, as well as anti-Nazi – yet it is clear that these positions would only be used as sticks to beat the Muslim community. It claimed to defend liberal British values against the purportedly intolerant religion of Islam.

Yet its claim that it was opposed only to 'militant Islam' was indefensible, as the EDL had been shown time and time again expressing bigoted and racist views of Muslims. Traditional far right groups, including neo-Nazi organisations, had clearly infiltrated the organisation – the reason given for the resignation of leader 'Tommy Robinson'[46] (himself a former BNP voter turned Ukip supporter) in the autumn of 2013. The EDL has since fragmented and several smaller groups of a similar nature have emerged in its absence. Anti-Islamic street movements remain a regular occurrence. In the South Yorkshire town of Rotherham alone, there were sixteen far right marches between 2012 and 2016.

The dangerous impact on public safety is best elucidated by the EDL and their brand of street protest. The League's demonstrations, which fused anti-Muslim politics with marches fired by alcohol, cocaine and violence, led to huge drains on police and local resources. For one demonstration alone in Rotherham, the cost was estimated by a local councillor to be £1 million in terms of police deployment and loss of trade for local businesses.[47] The damage to community cohesion is less easy to quantify. The fear felt by thousands of Muslims, their friends and families during EDL marches cannot be calculated. Here lies a misunderstood aspect of the far right – their ideas and activities, whilst marginal in the grand scheme of British life, have a disproportionate impact on a range of people and communities. To claim their lack of electoral success as evidence of their irrelevance is to be deeply naïve, and at worst, wilfully ignorant of the threats posed by far right ideology to ethnic and social minorities.

The most extreme and dangerous manifestation of the contemporary far right comes in the form of terrorism, and this threat has not waned in recent years. The most notable example comes from Norway, where in 2011, Anders Behring Breivik conducted a series of attacks. At around 3.30 p.m. on

22 July, Breivik detonated a homemade car bomb in the centre of the capital, Oslo. Eight people were killed and 209 injured. Following the bomb attack, Breivik, dressed as a policeman, drove to Utøya Island, where a camp was being hosted by the youth wing of Norway's governing Labour Party. Breivik massacred 69 people, mostly children and teenagers, and injured 110 with a semi-automatic assault rifle.

Breivik, who was captured by police on the island, claimed he was preventing the 'Islamisation' of Norway by killing its future implementers. He had established links to the European-wide counter-jihad movement. A 1,518-page manifesto written by him and uploaded online shortly before he conducted the attacks reveals a cocktail of racist, conspiratorial and ultra-nationalist views which are commonplace amongst the contemporary far right and even among more 'moderate' right-wing populist movements.

Having seen its own incident of far right terrorism in the 1990s with David Copeland, the threat has not disappeared in Britain in more recent years. A BNP candidate, Robert Cottage, was jailed in 2007 for the possession in his home of explosive chemicals, which police described as 'the largest amount of chemical explosive of its type ever found in this country'.[48] Martin Gilliard, a neo-Nazi, was jailed in 2008 when police discovered homemade nail bombs and other weapons, as well as a note stating: 'I am so sick and tired of hearing nationalists talk of killing Muslims, of blowing up Mosques, of fighting back . . . the time has come to stop the talk and start to act.'[49] As *New Statesman* columnist Medhi Hasan stated, 'terrorism, we know, is not the exclusive preserve or franchise of dark-skinned, bearded Muslims'.[50]

We have seen in this chapter how the political environment

in Britain during the first decade of the twenty-first century became toxified by the growth of the far right and the continued hysterical media coverage of immigration. Whilst the right-wing media were vehement in their criticism of the BNP, they had already opened the door to xenophobic politics. Their criticisms of the BNP, whilst denying the party legitimacy, rang hollow. The BNP were telling voters on the doorstep what they were reading in their newspapers.

Perceptive figures in the media recognised that the fascism-tainted BNP would always be doomed to failure. James Forsyth, writing for the *Daily Telegraph* shortly after Nick Griffin's appearance on *Question Time*, argued: 'The Griffin-led BNP won't become a serious political player. Griffin is too unattractive and his extremist statements too well documented for him to successfully reinvent himself.' Yet the party's anti-establishment message, aimed at an increasingly angry white working class, had clearly tapped into something bigger, and its constituency could not be ignored. Forsyth predicted accurately: 'If the political parties continue to forget or write off sections of the electorate then someone else, more plausible and with less baggage, will come along and seriously advance the BNP's vile agenda.'[51] Enter Ukip.

5
BREAKING POINT: ENTER UKIP

You know the one. It begins quite promisingly. The piano goes 'gurdle gurdle gurdle gurdle dum'. Then the dirge-like singing starts and the sugar-coated imperialism kicks in. Get rid of all your diverse human ambitions and passions (and so, presumably, art and personal loves and standards). Get rid of all your nations, possessions, faiths and loyalties (and so, presumably, families, languages and diversity in habitat, custom and culture), get rid, in short, of your identities and of everything that makes you human, and everything will suddenly be oh, so simple and lovely. The man might just have well has said, 'Why not kill yourselves while you're at it? That way you can be sure of peace.'

Nigel Farage on John Lennon's 1971 song 'Imagine'

Having witnessed the rise and fall of the BNP, we can now see how the palpable demand for an anti-immigration political movement was filled by Ukip. The party rose to become an important political player in the run-up to Brexit in an increasingly xenophobic and intolerant political climate. Ukip truly brought anti-immigration politics from the margins to the mainstream of British politics and significantly contributed to raising the issue of immigration prior to the Brexit vote. The Conservative Party began to ape Ukip's language and ceded to their demands for an EU referendum. Immigration became almost wholly seen by the political class as a problem which needed to be controlled. Whilst Ukip's influence on the Brexit campaign was marginal, without the party's prior rise, there may well have been a different outcome on 23 June 2016.

There is certainly plausibility in Nigel Farage's argument that Ukip reflects a more mainstream, less extreme outlet for anti-immigration politics than the BNP. As Farage himself says, 'We have nothing in common with the BNP. They are racist. We are inclusive. They are authoritarian. We are anti-authoritarian. They hate Europe, to be sure, as much as they hate the rest of the world and a large percentage of Britons. We love Europe but happen to reject the EU.'[1] There is much to quibble with in such a self-gratifying statement, but the rise of Ukip at the expense of the BNP on an anti-immigration platform will have come as a relief to many.

The BNP's collapse did not, however, represent a victory for liberalism or the defeat of intolerant ideas, but merely the rejection of a party with too much fascist baggage, which contributed heavily to its own downfall via infighting and poor financial management. Ukip's surge has not created a more tolerant Britain – far from it. Ultimately, the rise of the BNP was indicative that sections of the British public had grown increasingly prejudicial and angry, lazily blaming the problems associated with industrial decline, globalisation and modernity on immigrants, foreigners and the so-called 'political establishment'.

Yet the collapse of the BNP did not reflect the failure of this group to achieve a political voice, but the beginning of its ascendancy, as Ukip embarked upon a genuinely unprecedented electoral rise following the 2010 general election. We must therefore grapple with the moral quandary that although defeated, many of the BNP's ideas live on. Ukip ultimately represents the further mainstreaming of political xenophobia which polluted the national debate in the prelude to Brexit.

Cranks and gadflies

That Ukip rose to become a significant, radical right-wing populist party which would have a substantial impact on British politics was certainly not inevitable. It began as a single-issue party. Ukip's origins lie in the febrile debates over Britain's EU membership in the early 1990s, when Eurosceptic group the Anti-Federalist League was founded by Dr Alan Sked, a historian from the London School of Economics. Sked had previously stood as a candidate for the Liberal Party in 1970, but the Anti-Federalist League would quickly become a home for disgruntled Tories. After an ineffectual first two years, the party was rebranded as the United Kingdom Independence Party (Ukip) in 1993.

Ukip sought to recruit Eurosceptics from the right of the Conservative Party, who had seen a series of run-ins with leader and Prime Minister John Major, particularly over the Maastricht bill (which further integrated Britain into the European Community) in May 1992. Its early years would be fruitless – the party was severely prone to infighting and could not agree on an electoral strategy. At its first general election, its vote would be massively overshadowed by millionaire Sir James Goldsmith's lavishly funded Referendum Party – which essentially ran on the same issue of opposition to the European Union. The Referendum Party won over 800,000 votes, whereas Ukip got just over 100,000, a miserable 0.3 per cent of the vote.

They were to achieve something of a breakthrough in 1999

during the European parliamentary elections. Ukip benefited from the disbanding of the Referendum Party following Goldsmith's sudden death in 1997, both in terms of monopolising the Eurosceptic vote and attracting Referendum Party candidates. Profiting from the European proportional representation system, Ukip achieved around 7 per cent of the national vote, which gave them three seats in the European Parliament. The vote provided the party with publicity it had not previously enjoyed. One of Ukip's first MEPs, a young Nigel Farage, described his first Eurostar commute to his new place of work, beset by BBC cameras: 'We opened a bottle of champagne, partly just because we wanted to celebrate, partly because it gave us something to do with our mouths other than putting our inexpert feet in them and with our hands other than scratching, nose-picking or whatever.'[2]

Despite this clear success, the party remained beset by civil war and very nearly died. It remained essentially a single-issue party, desiring little more than an immediate withdrawal from the European Union, and had very little to say on anything else. Its general election performance would regularly be dismal, achieving 1.5 per cent in 2001, 2.2 per cent in 2005 and 3.1 per cent in 2010, and never coming close to winning a seat. Yet, continuing to benefit from the proportional European system, where seats are awarded according to the total percentage vote, it developed something of a specialism in picking up seats in the European Parliament. 2004 would see the party win over 16 per cent of the vote and twelve seats, while in 2009 it would finish second – ahead of Labour and the Liberal Democrats.

At this point, Ukip's focus on immigration was overshadowed by that of the BNP. The party's Euroscepticism ultimately guided its view on immigration and it continued to frame everything in terms of EU membership, arguing in its manifesto that 'the only people who should decide who can come to live, work and settle in Britain should be the British people themselves. We can only do this outside of the EU political union.'[3]

Although the party achieved a certain notoriety before 2010, particularly around European elections, its impact on British politics was minimal in the grand scheme of things. It developed a reputation as something of a political oddity. Conservative leader Michael Howard would refer to the party as 'cranks and political gadflies' and claimed its members had links to the far right. Speaking before the 2004 European elections, Howard told Tory activists in an internal briefing document: 'a UKIP vote is not just a wasted vote: it is a dangerous vote for useless representatives who will do next to nothing for their constituents'.[4] Similar attacks would be made by Howard's successor, when David Cameron described Ukip as 'fruitcakes, loonies and closet racists, mostly'.[5] Both insults would be embraced by Ukip: one can still purchase a 'Cranks and Gadflies tie' from Ukip's online shop and fruitcake is regularly on offer at Ukip party conferences.

Fruitcakes or not, senior figures in Ukip consistently exhibited madcap and bigoted behaviour. Godfrey Bloom was a Ukip MEP between 2004 and 2014. He once claimed in a TV interview that he 'doesn't do political correctness' and developed a particular reputation for controversy. In 2013, he referred to countries who received foreign aid as 'Bongo Bongo land'. In 2010, he was booted out of the chamber of the European Parliament for shouting 'Ein Reich, Ein Volk, Ein Führer!' at Martin Schultz, the German leader of the socialist parliamentary group. Bloom left the party in 2014. Another MEP, Janice Atkinson, referred to the Thai wife of a Ukip supporter as a 'ting tong from somewhere'. She was expelled from the party in 2015 after severe expenses fraud was uncovered.

Attempts to put down Ukip by the Conservative Party cannot be seen as surprising, given that the party's grassroots were overwhelmingly Eurosceptic and agreed with much of Ukip's rhetoric and policies. The party's core issue of Euroscepticism had grown in salience in British politics following the accession of the A8 countries in 2004, but also thanks to the Lisbon Treaty in 2009 and the Eurozone crisis. The treaty, which gave more powers to Brussels and further integrated Britain into the EU, had particularly drawn the ire of the party's base. David Cameron, in a bid to appease Eurosceptics, gave a 'cast-iron' pledge to offer a referendum on the treaty in 2007, before making a U-turn in 2009 as it became obvious he wouldn't be able to deliver it if elected. Cameron's strength on EU issues was permanently weakened following this 'betrayal'. Although Britain was not a member of the single currency, the Eurozone crisis gave the perception that the country was shackled to a Europe in economic chaos and decline. Ukip in particular benefited, and their wacky reputation began to appear irrelevant as they made electoral inroads.

The BNP had radicalised a significant proportion of the white working class towards anti-immigration politics. Ukip had been targeting former BNP voters for years, claiming, somewhat opportunistically, to be an anti-racist, anti-immigration party. Nigel Farage said in 2014 that Ukip sought to 'deal with the BNP question by going out and saying to the BNP voters: "if you are voting BNP because you are frustrated, upset, with the change in your community but you are holding your nose because you don't agree with their racist agenda, then come and vote for us" . . . And I would think that we have taken a third of the BNP vote from them, and I don't think that anyone has done more to damage the BNP than Ukip and I am quite proud of that.'[6] A cynic would argue that Farage was less concerned with destroying the far right and their ideas than incorporating their voters into Ukip.

The party began to show signs of strength in a series of by-elections in 2012, coming second in northern seats in Barnsley, Rotherham and Middlesbrough as well as at local elections. The party came a close second in a by-election in the south-east town of Eastleigh in 2013. One reason for this sudden surge in support is down to the fact that the Liberal Democrats, normally the benefactor of the 'none-of-the-above' vote, were now in a governing coalition with the Conservative Party. There had also clearly been a shift in the political landscape. Ukip and the Lib Dems were very different beasts, the latter being Britain's most Europhile and socially liberal party. Ukip were gaining a reputation as a party which sought to address Britain's rapidly growing concerns about immigration as well as one which looked to stick it to 'the establishment'. Their supporters also came from very different backgrounds, Ukip's tending to be less educated, more economically vulnerable and older.[7] Ukip would also soon become synonymous with its leader, Nigel Farage.

Farage, educated at the exclusive public school Dulwich College and a former city trader, was indeed a curious figure to lead an avowedly anti-establishment party. As *New Statesman* columnist Helen Lewis sarcastically noted: 'When Nigel Farage stood up in the European parliament to grandstand about how "virtually none of you have ever done a proper job in your lives", he was not an elite. But the Lithuanian cardiac surgeon behind him, born in a Gulag, was.'[8] Farage quickly developed a reputation as a loveable cad – a fag-smoking, beer-swilling man of the people. He was also an adept media performer, a populist who sought to speak directly to 'the people', particularly on subjects which he claimed 'the establishment' ignored – notably immigration. The party consistently began to poll above 10 per cent nationally, and developed a new role as Britain's 'third party'.

Populism: the people are always right

Why had Ukip begun to succeed now, having played only a minor role in British politics for much of its existence? One of the major reasons is its successful adoption of radical right-wing populism, which had been shown to be a successful strategy by similar parties on the far and radical right across Europe. Populism has been one of the major new political phenomena to appear since the end of the Cold War in western Europe and the United States. Populist parties have achieved varying degrees of success across Europe for many years and Ukip reflects the British expression of a wider right-wing backlash against mainstream politics.

Populism is a word deeply contested by academics and commentators. However, at an ideological level, according to Cas Mudde, Professor of Political Science at the University of Georgia and a leading academic expert on the subject, the populist radical right can be described as nativist and authoritarian.[9] Nativism is perhaps the most immediately discernible feature of radical right-wing populism. It is the idea that the promotion of the national interest should upstage all else. Nativism is most often accompanied by xenophobia and hostility towards 'outsiders' in a number of guises, be they ethnic minorities, immigrants, foreign leaders, or international organisations such as the EU.

Authoritarianism is the belief that society should be strictly ordered and transgressors should be punitively coerced into obeying. Authoritarian attitudes place a strong emphasis on governments combating crime and delivering strict punishments to its perpetrators. Authoritarianism is by no means limited to the radical right, and indeed left-wing as well as right-wing authoritarian states can be witnessed over the twentieth century.

The term populism itself is not well understood. Populism is the belief that society is ultimately divided into two distinct groups: 'the people' and a rotten, out-of-touch elite, and that politics should be guided by the will of 'the people'. Given the idea that the 'common sense' of 'the people' should prevail, there is a deep mistrust of government and in particular, of the independent political institutions fundamental to liberal democracy, which, for example, seek to safeguard rights for ethnic minorities to ensure their voices are heard. Radical right-wing populists are not opposed to democracy, but to *liberal* democracy, believing in majoritarian rule.

The most common expression of populism is anti-establishment and anti-elite rhetoric. The ideas that 'the establishment doesn't understand the concerns of ordinary people' or that 'the rotten establishment ignores the will of the people to further its own interests' have become common currency in European politics and are indicative of the rise of populism, both on the right and the left. Indeed, populism need not be exclusive to the radical right with a nativist and authoritarian bent. Anti-capitalist left-wing populism is also a significant political trend, particularly in southern Europe (e.g. governing Greek party Syriza who merge traditional class-struggle politics with populism).

The fact that populism can appear in a number of left-wing and right-wing forms means it can also be viewed as a political style, rather than as a distinct ideology.[10] It is perhaps the unique 'style' of right-wing populism which has afforded it so much attention. Right-wing populist parties often have flaboyant, charismatic leaders, such as Farage or Geert Wilders of the Dutch Party for Freedom. Both seek to present themselves as the voice of 'ordinary people' and the scourge of the 'political establishment'. They talk in the language of Everyman, in the case of Nigel Farage with a pint and a cigarette in hand. They are often slick media performers who utilise their platform to make direct appeals to people over issues which are presented as 'taboo', such as immigration, multiculturalism and Islam. They seek to establish an emotional connection with the public through inflammatory rhetoric and by 'saying the unsayable', all the time framing their language as 'common sense' and no different from what 'ordinary' people think.

The radical right places a huge emphasis on identity. Sarah de Lange, Professor of Political Science at the University of Amsterdam and an expert on the radical right in Europe, explains this worldview: 'Immigration is perceived as a problem because it encourages cultural diversity and threatens the norms and values of the host country.' The radical right also 'perceives globalisation and therefore Europeanisation as a problem for the same reasons – because it is at odds with the identity of the nation state'. The populist element of far right ideology 'perceives politics as corrupted by an elite that's not acting in the interests of ordinary people'. Whilst this can be seen across a range of countries, national traditions matter greatly when looking at the radical right in individual countries. 'The Netherlands has a very liberal tradition. The emphasis [from the radical right] is on Dutch identity as defined by liberal principles such as the equality between men and women, gay rights, freedom of speech. It sees Islam as conflicting with those traditions because it doesn't grant these rights.'[11]

Stefaan Walgrave, Professor of Political Science at the University of Antwerp and an expert in political communication, tells me that populism is ultimately a 'fierce critique of representative democracy'. He argues: 'It boils down to a very simple criticism that representatives, who should do what the people want them to do, don't do what they are supposed to do. So it is not a criticism of democracy per se. People's expectations with regard to democracy have changed.' The big question for Walgrave in explaining the populist surge is 'whether the people have changed or whether the representative system has changed'. He is critical of the argument that 'political systems are indeed less responsive and less reactive and representative systems are less concurrent with what the people want than they used to be' due to globalisation and EU integration. He believes that people have changed.

Political systems and policies are no less responsive than they used to be; according to Walgrave, 'we have changed'. Voters' political stances have become more specialised, and they have become increasingly dissatisfied with 'broad church' parties (such as the Labour Party) who try and incorporate a range of views. Voters are 'less loyal, we are more highly schooled, we are more sceptical. We don't feel represented. We don't have party identification as we had twenty years ago, so voter volatility is increasing. Political dissatisfaction that leads to populism is a deep-seated structural evolution. Not so much a political evolution, but a cultural shift.' He goes on to say: 'I've spoken to a lot of MPs in different countries, political elites – party leaders, ministers, Members of Parliament are *obsessed* with public opinion. They are constantly trying to feel what the people think. They want to be responsive because they think that if they won't be responsive then they will be punished electorally – it's an obsession.' He concludes, 'On the one hand you have the public saying "elites are not listening to us, they are not responsive" and on the other hand if you study those elites they are trying to be as responsive as they can.'[12]

A Coalition of problems

Whilst Ukip's populist strategy was successful, the wider climate greatly assisted them. Anti-refugee and anti-immigrant sentiment had, as we have seen, already become a prominent feature of Britain's political culture under the Labour government. Driven by a sensationalist media intent on selling newspapers and reporting drama rather than facts, immigration had become an increasingly significant issue for the general public. The 2010 general election was inconclusive, with neither the Conservatives nor Labour securing a majority. Britain either faced a potentially unstable hung Parliament – for the first time since the 1970s – or a coalition government, for the first time since 1945. An agreement between the Conservative Party and junior partner the Liberal Democrats ensured that the latter materialised. David Cameron, who had called for his party to 'stop banging on about Europe' early in his leadership, would be Prime Minister.

Cameron would face many of the same challenges as his New Labour predecessors, particularly over immigration. The Conservative Party manifesto from 2010 (which had the cringeworthy title 'An invitation to Join the Government of Britain') pledged to 'take net migration back to the levels of the 1990s – tens of thousands a year, not hundreds of thousands'.[13] It was a promise he simply could not keep, and it would come back to haunt him during the EU referendum campaign. Economic policies of austerity and spending cuts, which sought to reduce Britain's mammoth budget deficit, grew increasingly unpopular. The perception of Cameron and Osborne, alumni of Eton and Harrow respectively, cutting the nation's cloth certainly rankled.

A 2014 poll by YouGov demonstrated the scale of the increase in negative public attitudes towards politicians, with 48 per cent of respondents believing that they were 'out for themselves' and another 30 per cent seeing them as 'out for their party'. Only 10 per cent believed they wished to do what was right for the country. During the Second World War, the figure for those who believed politicians sought to do the best for their country stood at 36 per cent, and even during the tumultuous years of the 1970s, dropped only to around 28 per cent. Anti-politician sentiment has since increased significantly.[14]

The lack of trust in politicians was combined with a general pessimism over the future of the country – a difficult phenomenon to explain, but one which certainly grew after the financial crisis and the ensuing economic austerity. One poll conducted by Ipsos MORI in late 2013 found that just 20 per cent of the British public believed that young people would have a better life than their parents, with 54 per cent thinking things would be worse. Pessimism appeared to be particularly entrenched amongst young people. A mere 22 per cent of younger people in the country believed their life would be better than their parents', in contrast to 36 per cent of the country as a whole.[15]

Questions surrounding the European Union and immigration would loom large over the Coalition's five years in government. The period saw a continued rise in anti-immigration sentiment, as well as a new, insurgent populist party on the right. The rise of Ukip ramped up anti-immigration politics and neither the Conservatives nor Labour found themselves capable of containing it.

Feverish discussions of immigration, as always, often mushroomed into wider questions. This was a period when Britain's multicultural society would come under sustained attack by a coalition of hard right populists and the mainstream right. The role Ukip played in this must not be underestimated – suddenly, it appeared, in their own words, 'a non-racist, non-sectarian' party had enabled the country to discuss immigration sensibly. This misplaced notion opened the floodgates to debate the like of which had last been seen in Britain during the late 1960s and 70s.

We must emphasise the extent to which mainstream politicians, from New Labour to the Coalition government, opened the door for Ukip, whose national poll ratings had grown from 3 per cent at the 2010 election, to a consistent 10 per cent and upwards from early 2013. Politicians made a fatal error in how they responded to anti-immigration sentiment, which had a dramatic subsequent impact on how immigration politics was framed. They rarely challenged the idea that immigration was a 'problem' and frequently claimed to have it under control. Yet immigration from within the EU could not be controlled under freedom of movement rules, while immigration from outside the EU, under British jurisdiction, had proved hellishly difficult to control since the Second World War. Political sentiment, such as Cameron's pledge to cut immigration to the 'tens of thousands', was not merely unrealistic, it was dishonest. Ukip's claim that Britain could not control its immigration system whilst in the EU was, in part, correct. However, the response of the Coalition government was to deny this fact, which only added to the sense of mistrust amongst the public over how politicians were handling immigration.

David Feldman locates this problem historically. He notes the relationship between the immigration debate which followed Enoch Powell's speech and contemporary anti-immigration sentiment, pointing out that in the entire immigration debate following the Second World War, 'what has been largely absent is any coherent counter narrative' to the idea of immigration as a problem. 'A crucial variable is the extent to which that story has been challenged. It wasn't challenged very effectively in the decades when it was possible and promising to challenge that story and it is even harder now.'

Feldman reflects on the legacy of postwar immigration policy, noting that there has been, consistently, a 'tacit conspiracy to quell anti-immigration sentiment by successive governments saying: "we have got firm immigration laws and they are working"'. However, 'what was being said about immigration was palpably not true. The electorate had not been told the whole truth. There *were* increasing numbers and no one was actually saying to people "this is fine".' Feldman notes that 'there was the idea that "immigration is a bad thing" which might or might not be the case, but also "it's a bad thing and we are stopping it". It was being regulated but it wasn't being stopped.' This narrative 'created a situation which played into the hands of the likes of Ukip. It gave Farage an opportunity.'[16]

Fighting or aping Ukip?

Signs that British politics was moving towards the right appeared even before Ukip's rise. David Cameron launched a stinging attack on multiculturalism in his first speech on radicalisation and terrorism in 2011. Whilst Gordon Brown had criticised the notion during his leadership, his comments were levelled for the most part at the segregation allegedly caused by multiculturalism at community level. Cameron's argument went further, saying that multiculturalism had encouraged Muslims to drift towards extremism: 'Under the doctrine of state multiculturalism, we have encouraged different cultures to live separate lives, apart from each other and the mainstream. We have failed to provide a vision of society to which they feel they want to belong. We have even tolerated these segregated communities behaving in ways that run counter to our values.'

Cameron also appeared to endorse the view that white people were overzealously accused of being racist and treated differently from Muslims: 'When equally unacceptable views or practices come from someone who isn't white, we've been too cautious – frankly, even fearful – to stand up to them.'[17] Similar views were put forward by French and German leaders Nicolas Sarkozy and Angela Merkel, reflecting a continental centre right who increasingly appeared to be aping the language of the radical right. Yet there was something deeply insalubrious about Cameron's speech, which discussed issues surrounding the British Muslim community and integration at an international event called the Munich Security Conference.

The content was more carefully considered than right-wing tabloid rants about how multiculturalism was inevitably cultivating terrorists, yet its setting at a security event appeared to endorse the idea that, as the *Economist* argued, 'the presence of Muslims on British soil was essentially a question of national security and counter-terrorism'.[18] For all the nuance in the speech, the headlines were always going to focus on Cameron's emphasis on the failure of multiculturalism. An endorsement of such a position by the Prime Minister ultimately reflected the rapid descent of multiculturalism from an ideal in the 1990s and the first term of New Labour, to a cause upon which to lay the blame for poor race relations and terrorism.

The Conservative Party increasingly sought to mimic the rhetoric of Ukip in an attempt to appear in control of immigration. The year 2013 saw the rolling out of the sinister so-called 'go home vans', which displayed Home Office billboards stating 'Here illegally? Go home or face arrest'. The vans were condemned by the Conservatives' coalition partners and were scrapped before the end of the year. Not only did they fail to work (the vans only led to one voluntary repatriation), they were indicative of an increasingly desperate Conservative Party seeking to look tough on immigration.

Evidence was growing that Ukip were having a great impact on mainstream politics, despite a relatively modest election performance. Also growing in influence were the Conservative Party's right-wing backbenchers, who despised the compromises of coalition government and sought to use their significant voting influence to drag Cameron rightwards. Most importantly, these twin forces influenced Cameron's decision to offer a referendum on Britain's membership of the European Union in January 2013. A significant proportion of the Conservatives' parliamentary party had already demanded a referendum and a more Eurosceptic stance from Cameron. Ukip, who had a strong 2012, appeared to present a further significant electoral challenge to the Tories, one which could split the right-wing vote in marginal seats – potentially giving them to Labour.

Cameron also wanted to use the referendum as a means of taking Europe 'off the table', at least in the short term, giving him a freer hand in parliamentary votes which would no longer be jammed by irreconcilable Eurosceptics. Yet his pledge neither stymied the growth of Ukip nor appeased it. His backbenchers bemoaned his inability to enshrine the referendum pledge in law, following opposition from the government's coalition partners. Ultimately, using an EU referendum to counter flak from his right represented a doomed strategy from the beginning. As someone who fundamentally wanted to stay in the EU, he would never appease Britain's hard-line Eurosceptics: they would never be sated. As former Chancellor Ken Clarke, a cabinet minister under Cameron, put it, 'If you want to go feeding crocodiles then you'd better not run out of buns.'[19]

In late 2013, the Conservative Party sought to 'shoot the Ukip fox' just over six months before the European elections. Despite surely knowing that the party's pledge to cut immigration to the 'tens of thousands' was hopelessly unrealistic, David Cameron attempted to curb migration through the Immigration Bill. Introduced by Home Secretary Theresa May, the bill sought to clamp down on illegal immigration by creating, in May's own words, a 'hostile environment' for illegal immigrants and ensuring they were easier to deport.

The bill, which was largely comprised of trivial matters such as preventing 'sham marriages', also caved in to the widespread myth that immigrants were abusing social welfare through 'health tourism' (according to a government report, the cost of health tourism was estimated to be around £110–280 million annually, out of a total health budget of over £90 billion, making up barely 0.3 per cent of expenditure).[20] The shambolic bill – which both divided the Conservative Party and strained relations with its coalition partners – was voted through, but it did nothing to prevent Ukip picking up council seats and winning the 2014 European elections. As the now old saying goes – 'you cannot out-Ukip Ukip'.

Another case of the Conservative Party trying to talk tough on immigration came when immigration minister Mark Harper resigned for (ironically) employing an illegal immigrant as a cleaner. His replacement, James Brokenshire, immediately sought to make a name for himself as an immigration hawk, giving a speech to the think-tank Demos where he mimicked the language of Ukip: 'For too long, the benefits of immigration went to employers who wanted an easy supply of cheap labour; or to the wealthy metropolitan elite who wanted cheap tradesmen and services – but not to the ordinary, hard-working people of this country.'[21] Brokenshire drew derision from all sides. *The Times* columnist Matthew Parris described him as a 'startled mole of a junior minister morphed into a demented ferret', arguing that the Conservative Party appeared to be attacking its own voters in order to win over Ukip support.[22]

As the Conservatives were rocked in late 2014 by the defections of MPs Douglas Carswell and Mark Reckless to Ukip, it was becoming increasingly obvious that the party which had pledged to cut immigration had very little ammo against the Ukip phenomenon, other than trying to copy them. They were turning to increasingly desperate measures to try and allay fears over migration, as well as attempting to curb the numbers coming into Britain as net immigration remained high. Between 2011 and 2013, net immigration had hovered around the 200,000 mark – a consistently high level but lower than most years since 2003. In 2014 the figure reached a record high of 313,000.

Public opinion, already sceptical during Labour's time in office, moved even further against immigration during the Coalition's reign. In May 2011, YouGov found that 68 per cent of people were 'concerned that Britain is losing its own culture' and 73 per cent that 'Britain is already overcrowded'. In January 2012, should a hypothetical referendum be proposed on reducing net migration to zero, 69 per cent of respondents said they would vote in favour of it. Another YouGov poll in December 2012 showed that a huge majority of 67 per cent of the country believed that 'immigration over the last decade . . . had been a bad thing for Britain'. A mere 11 per cent thought it had been good. Eighty per cent of those polled supported David Cameron's pledge to reduce immigration to the tens of thousands.

These negative attitudes saw a majority within each major party: 79 per cent of Conservatives wanted net immigration to be zero, as did 64 per cent of Labour supporters and 54 per cent of Liberal Democrats.[23] There appeared to be a clear incentive for major parties, as well as Ukip, not only to refuse to tackle growing anti-immigrant sentiment, but to co-opt it. As voters were continually warned about higher levels of net migration in the press, particularly over the possibility of hordes of Romanians and Bulgarians arriving in 2014, 2013 saw anti-immigration sentiment rise still further. That year 57 per cent of the public ranked it among their top three concerns, a figure 11 per cent higher than the preceding year.[24]

Polling conducted by Tory peer Lord Ashcroft in 2013 similarly found increasing disquiet over immigration. In analysing the politics of immigration, his survey identified seven distinctive groups – the first four being overwhelmingly hostile.

Sixteen per cent were categorised under 'universal hostility'. These were people against all forms of immigration and tended to be working class, middle-aged and with limited education. A further 16 per cent were identified as having 'cultural concerns' – these were people who believed immigration had a negative impact on the UK, and were particularly troubled by the cultural change it brought about.

Fourteen per cent of respondents in Ashcroft's poll were classified as 'competing for jobs', reflecting those who believed migrants posed a threat to jobs and wages. Twelve per cent represented the 'fighting for entitlements' segment, indicating their anxiety over migrants competing with the indigenous population for public services and welfare. More than 90 per cent of all of these groups supported the Home Office's 'go home or face arrest' van. In summary, those who saw immigration overwhelmingly as negative added up to around 58 per cent of those polled – expressing a range of criticisms from cultural change to jobs, wages, welfare and public services. Many placed immigration at the top on their list of concerns which faced Britain, above the economy.[25]

Do the fears which underpin Britain's scepticism about the value of immigration stack up? A common refrain is that the country has no more room. A *Daily Express* headline in 2009 blared 'Keep out, Britain is Full Up', while a similar variant from the *Daily Star* apocalyptically shouted 'Britain full to bursting with immigrants'.[26] The reality is that Britain is not 'full up'. It has a declining population due to a decrease in birth rates and the vast majority of the country is still rural, unsettled, not yet built upon. Concerns that immigrants take jobs and are a drain on the welfare state were and remain unfounded, with only anecdotal evidence available to argue there is a significant problem. Whilst between 1995 and 2015 the numbers of immigrants from the EU tripled, the impact on wages was minuscule. Jonathan Portes of the National Institute of Economic and Social Research found that between 2004 and 2012, the impact of migration on wages of the semi-skilled 'has been about 1 per cent . . . with average wages in this sector of about £8 an hour, that amounts to a reduction in annual pay rises of about a penny an hour'.[27]

It is widely accepted by mainstream economists that immigration provides more economic benefits than costs. A study conducted by researchers at the London School of Economics after the vote to leave the European Union argued that falls in wages were largely attributable to the financial crisis, rather than to migration. In addition, EU migrants tended to be 'more educated, younger, more likely to be in work and less likely to claim benefits than the UK-born'. EU immigrants contributed more in tax than they took out in welfare and public services, contributing to the reduction of Britain's large budget deficit.[28] Rather than a drain, migrants have been an economic advantage to the country during a period of economic downturn accompanied by the long-term problem of an ageing population.

The increased concern over immigration cannot be decontextualised from the economic austerity which was being undertaken by the Coalition government at the time, David Feldman tells me: 'What immigration politics at an economic level feeds into is the idea that the economy is a zero-sum game,' the idea that 'If someone gains someone else loses. That actually runs contrary to the Keynesian premises on which the economy was run for most of the postwar decades. The Keynesian premise that for any given input you'll get more out for the extra economic activity it generates.' Before the financial crisis of 2007–8 'politicians were very hesitant to give that argument – to shout from the rafters that immigration was an economic boon – even though that's what New Labour believed. And after the crash, when we don't have Keynesianism any more, we have austerity – at that point the economy does look more like a zero-sum game. Therefore, immigration becomes a much harder thing to sell to the electorate.'[29]

The Romanian 'tide'

Let us now turn to migration from Romania and Bulgaria, which created a newly caustic immigration debate in Britain. The British press had something of an obsession with Romanians even prior to the country's accession to the EU in 2007. Unflattering and downright slanderous portrayals of Romanians were a regular occurrence. In August 2006, the *Daily Express* ran a story entitled 'Look out Britain, here we come', interviewing a family planning on moving to the UK. The sub-headline read: 'The Ion family are work-shy scroungers who live in a hovel. In a few months they will leave Romania for a life of luxury and a pension, over here. Is it any wonder people think we are a soft touch?' The article is indicative of how an increasingly xenophobic and personalised immigration discussion in the press depicted a family of Romanians. The article begins 'Gheorghe could do with a bath. And a shave. But then he has just woken up. It's two in the afternoon.' Speaking of his wife, 'long-suffering Ramona heaves herself up from her chair with the weariness of a woman who no longer seems to care what her family get up to.' Apparently Gheorghe's brother 'has filled [him] with wonderful stories about free health care, a welfare system that asks no questions'.[30]

Romanians were often portrayed as a dirty, unclean, disease-ridden people, in a similar manner to asylum seekers in the early 2000s or even migrants in the nineteenth and twentieth centuries. The important difference, however, was that Romania was about to become one of Britain's partners in the European Union and subject to EU laws guaranteeing the free movement of people. A headline story in the *Sunday Express* in August 2006 yelled 'Tories demand our borders be closed amid fears of HIV time bomb'. The article, written by political editor Julia Hartley-Brewer – now a prominent radio talk show host – spoke of an 'HIV explosion in Romania and neighbouring Eastern European countries' which threatened 'to engulf the EU in a health time bomb as deadly as the Aids crisis afflicting Africa'.[31] It is difficult to imagine a story better designed to invoke fear and scapegoating of immigrants. Politicians from different sides, particularly Britain's insurgent radical right party, joined in gleefully.

The Migration Observatory at Oxford University found that in one year between December 2012 and December 2013 (with the removal of transitional controls which temporarily restricted immigration from Romania and Bulgaria still over a year away), nineteen national newspapers in Britain published over 4,000 articles and letters relating to Romanians and Bulgarians alone, averaging just under eleven per day. When stories were published, they focused overwhelmingly on issues relating to crime and anti-social behaviour. Some of the most common words appearing in such stories were 'criminal', 'beggar', 'gang', 'thief' and 'squatter'.[32]

Anti-immigration rhetoric had reached new depths in the run-up to 1 January 2014, when transitional controls would expire. Hysterical depictions of swarthy Romanian and Bulgarian hordes flocking to Britain in their millions were

conjured. In June 2014, Ukip would win the European parliamentary elections on an explicitly anti-immigration ticket.

The notion of Romanians as criminals was particularly
floated by Ukip. During the 2013 Eastleigh by-election, candidate Diane James (who narrowly finished second and would go
on to be elected Ukip leader in September 2016, only to resign
from the party a matter of weeks later) sought to exploit scaremongering about Romanian immigration for votes. She said,
'On 1 January 2014 the floodgates will open for Bulgarian and
Romanian citizens [to come to Britain]. We are not just talking about pressure on services from immigration but also,
and I have to say it, the crime associated with Romanians.'
Explaining her point, James went on, 'One of the problems with
the Olympics last year was the Metropolitan Police having to
deal with Romanian criminal gangs pick-pocketing.'[33] Not to
be outdone, party leader Nigel Farage would bellow at the Ukip
party conference later in the year that London was 'already
experiencing a Romanian crime wave'. Farage spoke of Britain
having 'open doors' to twenty-nine million people, ludicrously
implying all those able to would come.[34]

A short documentary for Channel 4 News presented eye-
opening insight into Farage's ability to ignore basic facts when
it came to migration. On a trip to Bulgaria, Farage was filmed
meeting leaders of the local Roma community, who said it was
unlikely they would move to Britain – complaining about the
weather and saying that Bulgaria was their home. Regardless,
he told the documentary producer, 'I don't know, but if I was a
young member of the Roma community, whatever the family
unit or traditions, I'd be getting out.' Farage spoke to a group of
university graduates in Sofia. He couldn't find a single one planning on moving to Britain, and one was offended by Farage's

claim that if he was Bulgarian he would leave. At the end of this 'fact-finding' mission, where he didn't appear to find anyone wishing to move, Farage concluded that it had reinforced his view 'that we are at risk from a second substantial migratory wave . . . logic says that quite a lot of them still will come'.

Headlines in 2013 spoke of 'Mafia bosses who can't wait to flood Britain with beggars', of 'countless would-be immigrants planning to move to Britain' from Romania and Bulgaria Implying like Farage that millions would potentially be arriving, an article in the *Daily Mail* stated that 'all 29 million citizens of Bulgaria and neighbouring Romania . . . will finally gain unrestricted rights to live and work in Britain'.[35] Stories covering destitute Romanians planning on coming to Britain were frequent, often portraying Romania as a post-apocalyptic hell hole where people were rushing for the exits. Pictures of Romanians with amputated limbs living in unmitigated squalor were splashed across the pages of the *Daily Mail* under headlines such as 'We want to get into your country before someone locks the door'.[36]

Patrick O'Flynn, political editor of the *Daily Express*, described the removal of controls (before they had been lifted) as an 'immigration calamity' and made completely unfounded claims that Romanians were coming for welfare alone, even comparing them unfavourably with Polish migrants: 'Migrants from Poland have been characterised by high labour market participation rates (that's jargon for "hard workers") and fairly low welfare dependency, there is every reason to fear that the reverse will be true of arrivals from Romania and Bulgaria.'[37] O'Flynn would give up his career in journalism in 2014 when he was elected as a Ukip MEP. The *Express* had effectively become Ukip's voice in the media.

In the days leading up to 1 January 2014, the media continued to pump out scare stories over the impending 'invasion'. The *Daily Star* ran headlines such as 'Immigrants to flood schools and hospitals'.[38] Romanian migrants were allegedly coming to 'take advantage of Britain's blossoming economy' according to the *Daily Express*. Interviewing Romanian MP Aurelian Mihai, the *Express* paraphrased him as saying that Romanians were coming from recession-hit countries in the Mediterranean, particularly as they had 'no access to unemployment benefits'. When Mihai was actually quoted, he stated that 'Romanians want a chance to work and be paid like anyone else . . . and use that to create better lives back home' and dismissed claims that benefits were the main draw factor.[39] When the controls were lifted, the media flooded to Stansted Airport to view this 'influx' of Romanians, only to find that the majority arriving were actually in fact working in Britain and returning from visits home.

One slightly baffled looking Romanian who had arrived for the first time, Victor Spiresau, told reporters, 'I don't come to rob your country. I work and then go home.' The *Daily Star* reported that 'Romanians top UK crime list . . . before they've even arrived' and that there were '[growing] fears of a crime wave last night as hordes of Romanians and Bulgarians bought every seat on planes and buses to the UK'. Tory MP Philip Hollobone reciprocated this view, arguing that 'We are importing a wave of crime from Romania and Bulgaria. Romanians are seven times more likely to be arrested in London than a British national.'[40] When migration figures came out a year later, it transpired that there was no invasion. An additional 22,000 Romanians and Bulgarians entered in 2014 – a minuscule amount.

Although the numbers failed to bear out the predictions of Ukip and the media, Romanian and Bulgarian immigration would feature heavily in the 2014 European elections. Nigel

Farage's deft ability to criticise immigration regularly and fervently whilst countering accusations of extremism was one of the main attributes of his success. The mask slipped, however, during a particularly tough grilling by James O'Brien on LBC Radio shortly before the election.

Farage, who at the time had a German wife, had been highlighting the alleged scourge of Romanian criminality and was asked by O'Brien what the difference was between having Germans (like his family) or Romanians as neighbours. Farage replied, sinisterly, 'You know what the difference is.' In a statement afterwards, he added that 'Any normal and fair-minded person would have a perfect right to be concerned if a group of Romanian people suddenly moved in next door.'[41] Labour leader Ed Miliband described the comments as a 'racial slur' and 'deeply offensive', while MP Keith Vaz observed that such language was similar to the abuse received by Asians in the 1960s and 70s. The incident proved not to jeopardise Ukip's success in the 2014 elections, an election in which they had over-performed on several occasions before – and the party swept to victory, claiming just short of 27 per cent of the vote and thirteen seats in the European Parliament.

The media's darling

The response of the media to Ukip's rise must be considered, as it could not be more different from their treatment of the BNP. Whilst the BNP were demonised as fascist, racist and dangerous, Ukip, and in particular Nigel Farage, were celebrated as a breath of fresh air. Farage, despite never holding political office in the UK and failing to be elected to Parliament on no less than seven occasions, was given an unprecedented platform on television in particular. He had appeared on the BBC's flagship political debate programme *Question Time* thirty-one times by 2017 – making him the eleventh most regular panel member in the history of a show which began in 1979.

Beyond providing completely disproportionate airtime for Ukip, there was significant collaboration – both formal and informal – between the party and the anti-immigrant press. The *Daily Express* endorsed Ukip in 2014 and its owner, Richard Desmond, would donate significant amounts of money to the party. More significantly, other tabloids continued to produce stories that confirmed Ukip's message: ideas that the EU was totalitarian, immigration was out of control, that there was a politically correct elite stifling debate and that multicultural-ism was a threat to British identity.

Newspaper columnists would leap to Farage's defence fol-lowing his regular inflammatory comments. After Farage was criticised for several remarks made in a Channel 4 documen-tary, 'Things We Won't Say About Race Which Are True', where he spoke of a Muslim 'fifth column' in Britain and called for the Race Relations Act to be repealed, Richard Littlejohn argued in the *Daily Mail*, 'Nigel Farage finds himself embroiled in yet another bogus race row simply for having the audacity to challenge the cosy consensus of our arrogant political elite.' Farage 'wasn't being racist, he was stating the bleedin' obvi-ous'. Littlejohn even aped the 'anti-establishment' attitude of Ukip: 'The political establishment doesn't want to hear that kind of dissent, however, so they try to drown out the debate with howls of racism. They have a vested interest in pretending Britain is a deeply racist society, even though we're far and away the most tolerant nation in Europe.'[42]

Littlejohn repeatedly came out in defence of Ukip, seeking to legitimise them as an important voice in public debate. He argued shortly before the local elections in 2013, 'Farage may come across as a bit of a circus act, but he speaks for millions of people who feel utterly disenfranchised by the political system . . . I wouldn't blame anyone who votes for UKIP this week, if that's what it takes to get the attention of the cosy little cartel at Westminster.'[43] Such rhetoric in favour of a radical right party, whose main campaigning weapon was anti-immigration politics and xenophobia, cannot be seen as surprising given the tabloids' increasingly hostile stance on immigration and multiculturalism since the turn of the twenty-first century, yet it differed entirely from responses to the BNP.

Hard right journalist Simon Heffer, writing in the *Daily Mail*, lavished praise on Farage's charisma, describing him as a 'technicolor man in a monochrome political class. To the chattering classes, his brash, confident, matey, plain-spoken persona makes him something of a demon. But to millions of voters he's someone with whom they can identify . . . When stuffy pundits sneer at his saloon-bar-and-fags image, he chuckles with the confidence of a man who knows that he, and not they, is in tune with the British people.'[44]

Other columnists similarly encouraged Ukip and Farage, at times even playing up the party's chances of achieving power. Kelvin Mackenzie, former editor of *The Sun*, following the *Charlie Hebdo* attack in January 2015, was to argue that if a similar event occurred in Britain in the run-up to the general election, 'Nigel Farage would be forming the next government . . . This country is on the edge and only needs a slight push to go over.'[45]

Melanie Phillips, writing in *The Times*, similarly mimicked the language of Ukip, claiming that 'LibLabCon' (a pejorative acronym used by Ukip to describe the three allegedly indistinguishable main political parties) were running scared of Ukip following their victory in the European elections. 'The Ukip fox is in the Westminster hen house; headless chickens doesn't even begin to describe the result.'[46] Ukip found many friends in the British press, and not just in the right-wing tabloids. Left-leaning newspaper the *Independent* provided Farage a weekly platform via a column in 2013. Editor Amol Rajan defended the decision amid criticism, and did not appear unduly concerned by its potential impact in normalising Ukip's anti-immigration politics: 'The sheer number of Ukip voters, and their likely triumph in the European elections in May, means your newspaper must choose between ignoring and engaging with them.'[47]

Nigel Farage is too clever to genuinely underestimate the impact the right-wing press had on his and Ukip's success, not just by defending him and the party, but through the continued proliferation of hysterical stories about immigration being 'out of control' and the failure of a politically correct establishment to stem it. Yet he appeared ungrateful for the significant platform his party and their views had been given. In the documentary 'Meet the Ukippers', broadcast in 2015, in which a Ukip councillor stated, 'I don't know why, but I don't like negroes or anyone with negro features,' Farage claimed the right-wing press were against Ukip. He spoke of the 'hatred of the tabloid press against us' and their role in increasing the perception of Ukip as racist. In 2017, speaking with chat show host Piers Morgan, Farage referred to the 'liberal media' who had 'attempted to demonise me and give me a bad name'. He went on, 'Will I ever forgive the British media for what they've done to me? No.'

The reality is that Farage owes his new-found position as a

global celebrity to the British media, who normalised his hard-line stance on immigration and his party's xenophobia. In contrast to the BNP, the right-wing press did not show a shred of anxiety over the rise of this anti-immigration party. One of Farage's great achievements was that he was able to avoid being labelled a 'fascist' or extremist – something that most radical critics of immigration since the Second World War have been accused of. Ukip's politics, whilst less extreme, nevertheless had xenophobia at its core, won votes by demonising foreigners and made paranoid criticisms of a decadent establishment in a very similar manner to the far right.

Then, just two years after Ukip's success in winning a national election in May 2014, we faced the Brexit vote.

6
TAKE BACK CONTROL: THE EU REFERENDUM

Napoleon, Hitler, various people tried this out, and it ends tragically. The EU is an attempt to do this by different methods.

Boris Johnson on the European Union,

May 2016

At the 2015 general election, Ukip would win just under 3.9 million votes, a dramatic increase on their 2010 total. If Britain had a proportional electoral system, as is the norm in continental Europe, they would have achieved around eighty seats. Under first-past-the-post, they were rewarded with just one. The Green Party – railing against government austerity and proposing a radical left-wing programme – achieved just under 1.2 million votes nationwide and were, like Ukip, rewarded with just one seat. Turnout saw an increase on 2010's figure, but still over a third of the country did not vote. The picture of the 2015 election was a mixture of anger and apathy, but one in which business as usual won through.

Whilst having a relatively typical outcome – a Conservative majority – results demonstrated significant signs of an ongoing revolt in British politics. The Scottish National Party took a sledgehammer to Scotland's political map, capturing all but three of Scotland's fifty-nine available parliamentary seats and achieving 50 per cent of the vote in the country. In doing so, they laid waste Labour's biggest stronghold and consigned them to an increasingly futile role north of the border.

During the general election campaign, anti-immigration politics had become increasingly normalised. Nigel Farage had been invited to the televised national debates and did not waste the opportunity to scapegoat immigrants for the problems facing Britain. To an audience of millions, he complained of HIV positive migrants coming to the UK and costing the NHS thousands of pounds per patient.

The print media also appeared to provide a platform for increasingly extreme voices. Katie Hopkins, a former contestant in the TV series *The Apprentice*, penned an article in her regular *Sun* column expressing incalculable callousness towards desperate refugees seeking sanctuary in Europe. In the week preceding the article, a boat carrying refugees in the Mediterranean sank, killing around 400 men, women and children. Hopkins said:

> NO, I don't care. Show me pictures of coffins, show me bodies floating in water, play violins and show me skinny people looking sad. I still don't care . . . Make no mistake, these migrants are like cockroaches. They might look a bit 'Bob Geldof's Ethiopia circa 1984', but they are built to survive a nuclear bomb. They are survivors. . . . It's time to get Australian. Bring on the gunships, force migrants back to their shores and burn the boats.[1]

Just days after the article was published, another boat sank, this time killing around 800.

Europe in flames

Economic problems relating to the single currency and indebted nations in southern Europe – particularly Greece – continued in 2015. Predictions of the economic collapse of Greece and the ensuing destruction of the euro were an almost daily occurrence. Terrorist attacks shocked the world, beginning with the brutal gun attack in Paris on the offices of satirical magazine *Charlie Hebdo*. The two perpetrators, who murdered twelve innocent people, were French Islamists who pledged allegiance to Al Qaeda's Yemeni cell. The scapegoating of Muslims across Britain following the actions of these extremists grew, as they had done after 9/11 and 7/7.

Nigel Farage sought to exploit the atrocity by using it as evidence of the failure of multiculturalism and argued, with inflammatory guile, that Britain had turned a 'blind eye' to 'fifth columnists' within the country. He used the attacks to further scapegoat the British Muslim community following the grooming scandal in Rotherham: 'You've only got to look in the north of England and the sexual grooming of young children to see admissions from public figures that they didn't bother to turn over the stone when they heard rumours of things going wrong, for the fear they might be thought to be racist.'[2]

Another shocking terror attack occurred on the night of 13 November. A combination of suicide bombings and gunfire, the deadliest occurring at an Eagles of Death Metal concert at the Bataclan Theatre, again in Paris, saw 130 massacred – 89 of them killed in the theatre. The impact of the attacks was certainly felt in Britain and heightened tensions among the public. Farage again used the atrocity as a means to attack ethnic minorities, claiming that there was 'a problem with some of the Muslim community in this country' and that evidence showed there was a 'tremendous conflict and a split of loyalties'. His comments were little different from those made about the British Jewish community by the far right before and shortly after the Second World War. He went on to say: 'I think we've reached a point where we have to admit to ourselves, in Britain and France and much of the rest of Europe, that mass immigration and multicultural division has for now been a failure.'[3]

The November attacks were the bloodiest act of violence since the Nazi occupation of France in the Second World War. The terrorists, nine in number, belonged to terror organisation Islamic State of Iraq and Syria (ISIS) – the ultra-Islamist pseudo-state which had conquered swathes of land in war-ravaged Syria and western Iraq. All the terrorists had fought in Syria for ISIS, some arriving with the masses of refugees seeking sanctuary in Europe. It would be this refugee crisis which the attackers sought to exploit, providing the biggest indicator to many of a continent out of control.

The civil war in Syria, a product of the Arab Spring which had been ongoing since 2011, had led to one of the largest humanitarian crises of the twenty-first century. Tens of thousands had been killed, millions displaced, all caught between the fighting factions of the Syrian rebels, the Assad regime and ISIS. In the summer of 2015, migration by sea increased dramatically. By the end of the year, a million refugees had arrived in Europe, the vast majority travelling through Turkey, via Greece and the Balkans. Over 350,000 Syrians had come to Europe, but the figures also included those from violence-stricken Iraq and Afghanistan, Kosovo, Albania and those fleeing other despotic regimes such as that of Eritrea. The migrant crisis had divided Europe between those who favoured a welcoming response and countries who responded with anger and fear to the so-called 'migrant invasion'.

Criticisms of Angela Merkel's welcoming stance led to a huge surge in far right support across Europe, particularly in Germany, the Netherlands, France and Austria. Its presence was felt significantly during the EU referendum. In February 2016, former Tory leader Iain Duncan Smith, Work and Pensions Secretary between 2010 and early 2016, openly claimed a link between refugees and terrorism. He argued that staying in the EU would make Britain vulnerable to Paris-style terrorist attacks, due to the fact that migrants entering Europe would be able to freely enter the UK: 'I think the present status of the open border we have right now, many of us feel does actually leave the door open and we need to see that resolved.'[4]

Nigel Farage's comments on the refugee crisis were identical to the kind of rhetoric witnessed in the British tabloids since the 'asylum panic' in the early 2000s. Farage warned that the EU had 'opened the door to an exodus of biblical proportions'. He also pushed the widely reported notion that refugees were 'bogus', describing the influx as 'illegal immigration'. He argued, 'We've lost sight of what is a genuine refugee.'[5]

Even the more highbrow broadsheets gave voice to those seeking to raise hysteria over the migrant crisis. Melanie Phillips, writing for *The Times*, argued against letting refugees into Britain, as it would 'alter the cultural balance of the country for ever'. Her explanation for the crisis was somewhat apocalyptic and perpetuated the notion of a 'migrant invasion', using the language of the far right: 'The Arab and Muslim world is disintegrating into chaos, war and terror. The ascendancy of radical Islam is producing untold barbarism. The West-imposed model of the nation-state is collapsing into tribal warfare. A dying culture has turned murderously upon itself whilst trying simultaneously to conquer the wider world.'[6] The idea that refugees were covert terrorists was further perpetuated. One *Daily Mail* cartoon, reminiscent of anti-Semitic Nazi propaganda, pictured Muslim men in traditional dress crossing a border sign, entitled 'Welcome to Europe: Our Open Borders and the Free Movement of People', along with women in burkas, rats and a man with an assault rifle.[7]

The referendum approaches

Given the right-wing political culture which had been developing in Britain for years, immigration was always likely to be a central issue of the EU referendum. Speaking in January 2017, Labour MP Dan Jarvis told me: 'The debate on immigration leading up to and during the EU referendum unleashed a range of political forces. As a part of that, things were said and language was used much more commonly than has been heard in this country for generations.' Most significantly, in terms of people's attitude to immigrants and those of different races and religions. Jarvis was candid: 'The currency of our national debate feels to me far less tolerant than it was even a year ago, and certainly a couple of years ago. The risk for those of us who are concerned about that is that it becomes a truth, an accepted wisdom – a normality.'[8] I now want to focus on how Brexit, arguably the greatest ever political achievement of the radical right in Britain, was achieved within this fetid atmosphere.

Electoral politics was clearly becoming more vicious and racialised. Just one month before the EU referendum, Sadiq Khan was elected London mayor in a highly charged battle with

Conservative Zac Goldsmith, who sought to exploit fears over Khan's Muslim faith. In a column in the *Daily Mail*, Goldsmith attacked Khan, claiming that he 'repeatedly legitimised those with extremist views'; the piece was accompanied by a picture of the London bus which had its roof ripped off on 7/7 by a suicide bomber. Khan would appear an odd person to attack as an extremist, given that he had voted for gay marriage in 2013 (and received death threats from actual extremists for doing so).

The referendum, held over a month later, began much like a general election – with the focus on the economy, namely the financial impact of leaving the EU. When the official Vote Leave campaign recognised this was an issue they could not conceivably win on, considering the swell of business opinion against Brexit, the debate dramatically shifted to immigration. Yet the campaign would not be dominated by Nigel Farage but by mainstream figures in the Conservative Party – Boris Johnson and Michael Gove – who lined up to attack their own government's record on immigration.

Vote Leave made immigration an issue with an open letter signed by, among others, Gove and Johnson. The letter was a direct attack on David Cameron's government, asserting that the failure to meet their target of cutting immigration to the tens of thousands was 'corrosive of public trust'. It also sought to link immigration with terrorism, claiming it was 'bad for security' as well as for the migrant crisis, stating that 'the EU's policies are failing in humanitarian terms . . . a vote to remain is a vote for the UK to continue supporting the EU's failed policies to deal with the tragic crisis in the Mediterranean'.[9] This ambiguous statement clearly had very little to do with Britain's membership of the EU, given the UK's exemption from EU asylum rules. It was designed to link EU membership with all forms of migration – asylum, refugees and economic migration – from both the Middle East and the EU.

More evidence of this strategy comes from Vote Leave's consistent but erroneous scaremongering over Turkey's bid to join the European Union. One billboard, coloured bright red, blared: 'Turkey (population 76 million) is joining the EU', alongside an illustration of footsteps leading through a door shaped like a British passport. A leaflet showed a map of countries 'set to join the EU', again coloured in red. All the other countries were greyed out except Iraq and Syria, which were shaded in pink. This was clearly designed to link freedom of movement with Turkey, a Muslim country, as well as Iraq and Syria, fellow Muslim countries, which had seen untold turmoil and were home to ISIS.

Another poster, which exploited a proposed visa-free travel arrangement between the EU and Turkey (which Britain wasn't even part of, as it isn't in the Schengen Area), claimed 'Britain's new border is with Syria and Iraq'. Defence Minister Penny Mordaunt stated that Britain did not have a veto over Turkish membership, which was completely false. David Cameron responded by arguing, 'It is not remotely on the cards that Turkey is going to join the EU any time soon. They applied in 1987. At the current rate of progress, they will probably get round to joining in about the year 3000 according to the latest forecasts.'[10]

Vote Leave argued that Turkey would bring little other than crime and death in the event that it achieved EU membership. They argued that it would 'create a number of threats to UK security. Crime is far higher in Turkey than the UK. Gun ownership is also more widespread. Because of the EU's free movement laws, the government will not be able to exclude Turkish criminals from entering the UK.'[11]

Joe Mulhall is clear about the implications of Vote Leave's

discourse on Turkey. 'When Michael Gove is talking about the criminality of Turks – this is racist rhetoric coming from main-stream, centre-right politicians. The reason they said "don't let in Turkey" was very clear – because they are Muslims. Some of it was veiled, some of it wasn't.' Ultimately, 'we mustn't see Brexit as some kind of far right coup and it was they who won the referendum – the reality is far scarier'.[12]

Farage, not to be outdone, would go down in infamy for the most inflammatory exploitation of immigration and the migrant crisis during the EU referendum. On the morning of 16 June, he unveiled a poster which showed swathes of deso-late-looking Muslim refugees arriving in columns on the trail through Slovenia into Croatia. Below, it said: 'Breaking point – the EU has failed us all', and 'we must break free of the EU and take back control of our borders'. The poster was clearly designed to give the impression that swathes of brown-skinned foreigners were trekking towards Britain's 'open borders'.

The 'Breaking Point' poster disgusted people on both the Remain and Leave sides. Yvette Cooper compared it to Nazi propaganda. Even Michael Gove said he 'shuddered' when he saw it. The poster, however, will also be remembered for what happened later on the day of its unveiling. Jo Cox, Member of Parliament for Batley and Spen, a Remain campaigner and an advocate of migrants' rights, was stabbed and shot by an extreme right terrorist outside her constituency surgery and died later that day. The attacker, Thomas Mair, was heard by onlookers to have shouted 'Put Britain first.' When he arrived in court for the first time he gave his name as 'death to traitors, freedom for Britain'. The relationship between this unspeak-ably tragic act and the climate in which it was committed was lost on few commentators.

Less than a week before the EU referendum, journalist Nick Cohen wrote in *The Guardian*: 'The English air is as foul as it has been at any point since my childhood. It is as if the sewers have burst. The Leave Campaign has captured the worst of England and channelled it into a know-nothing movement of loud mouths and closed minds.'[13] Describing 16 June and Jo Cox's death as 'a day of infamy', an impassioned article from *The Spectator*'s Alex Massie read:

> BREAKING POINT, it screamed above a queue of dusky-hued refugees waiting to cross a border. The message was not very subtle: Vote Leave, Britain, or be over-run by brown people. *Take control. Take back our country.* You know what I mean, don't you: *If you want a Turk – or a Syrian – for a neighbour, vote Remain.* Simple. Common sense. Innit? ...
>
> When you shout BREAKING POINT over and over again, you don't get to be surprised when someone breaks. When you present politics as a matter of life and death, as a question of national survival, don't be surprised if someone takes you at your word. You didn't make them do it, no, but you didn't do much to stop it either.
>
> Sometimes rhetoric has consequences. If you spend days, weeks, months, years telling people they are under threat, that their country has been stolen from them, that they have been betrayed and sold down the river, that their birthright has been pilfered, that their problem is they're too slow to realise any of this is happening, that their problem is they're not sufficiently mad as hell, then at some point, in some place, something or someone is going to snap. And then something terrible is going to happen.[14]

Cox's fellow Labour MP Stephen Kinnock, with tears in his eyes, told a special sitting of Parliament: 'Rhetoric has consequences . . . when insecurity, fear and anger are used to light a fuse, then an explosion is inevitable.' Nigel Farage, on his victory lap after it became clear Leave had won the referendum, barely a week after the death of Cox, nevertheless claimed that Brexit had been achieved 'without having to fight, without a single bullet fired'.

7

THE DECLINE OF ENGLAND

· *While Yarmouth enjoys an annual influx of chavs on their holidays,*
meaning that there's someone new to nick hub-caps from,
Lowestoft has more than enough of its own to fill the B&Bs turned
doss-houses on the sea-front and the hectares of council estates
that ring the town. Proof of how chav-friendly the place is can be
found in the fact that failing councils all over England (Liverpool,
Hackney, Portsmouth etc.) send their most delinquent families to
Lowestoft and slip the council a few quid for taking them off their
land. In Lowestoft, it's no longer enough to be 19 and have 3 kids to
get on the housing list – you now need at least 2 ASBOs.

Written by anonymous poster on
'iLiveHere – Britain's Worst Places to Live'

Which were the towns and cities whose inhabitants voted
in such numbers to leave the European Union? And why did
they vote such a way? We now turn to 'Brexitland' – the areas
which voted to leave in their droves – in order to understand
the Brexit vote at a more local level. We can see how a mistrust and hatred of elites, fears over immigration and an
overall sense of decline propelled the Brexit side to victory.
Criticism of immigration was one element of a wider feeling that the government did not understand the concerns of
ordinary people. This had been brewing for at least a decade,

as voters began turning away from the major parties.

We will see how areas which voted in the highest numbers to leave the EU saw it as a means to 'stick a finger up' at the government and vent their frustration over the way the country was headed. There was, and is, a growing belief that the country is going in the wrong direction, steered by an out-of-touch establishment. People's daily lives have become more of a struggle, things have got worse and above all, there is a great pessimism over the future.

Whilst overall attitudes to immigration were becoming more negative, there was also a growing internal divide within Britain over the subject. People with university degrees, those on higher incomes and ethnic minorities tended to be more favourable to immigration, whereas older, white Britons with fewer qualifications and lower incomes seemed more likely to be opposed. A Migration Observatory report showed that 65 per cent of those aged fifty and above favoured reducing immigration 'a lot', whereas 51 per cent of respondents aged 16–29 did. People earning under £20,000 per year were far more in favour of reducing migration than those earning over £30,000.[1] Reasons for opposition to immigration tend to divide academics and politicians. However, cultural factors tend to be a more accurate indicator of opposition than income. Many of these exact divisions would be exposed in Britain's vote to leave the European Union.

Those in areas of high immigration (such as London) and with friends of different ethnic and religious backgrounds tend to have more positive attitudes towards immigration, as opposed to those who stick to their traditional social circles. Many of the latter see immigration as a threat to their 'group' or national identity and are consequently more likely to be opposed to it. The importance of economic factors divides academics. Whilst those on a lower income tend to be more against immigration, it is still difficult to draw a causal link between being opposed to immigration and an individual's economic circumstances.[2]

Left behind

What is undoubtedly true is that many of those who voted to leave the European Union lived in towns and cities which had been experiencing economic and industrial decline for decades. If we go back to 1945, Britain delivered a landslide for the Labour Party on a radical socialist platform. Key industries such as coal and steel were nationalised. Britain possessed a world-class manufacturing industry which accounted for a third of national output and employed around 40 per cent of the total workforce. Twenty per cent of world exports in the 1950s and 60s were British. Whilst we should be wary of looking back on the period with rose-tinted glasses – as we have already seen, social and racial attitudes were often appalling – life was undoubtedly more prosperous for the working class in the first three decades that followed the Second World War. The trade union movement provided millions of workers with political representation. Tight-knit communities were forged around industrial areas based upon solidarity with one another.

Industrial decline began to bite in the 1970s as manufacturing firms started to collapse and become unprofitable due to mismanagement and foreign competition. Margaret Thatcher's government sped up the process by unleashing market forces upon nationalised industries through deregulation and privatisation. Workplaces and institutions which had become a core part of local identity disappeared into the dustbin of history. Unemployment, seen as a social evil for much of the postwar period, increased and particularly affected former industrial towns and cities. Whilst the impact on such areas was principally economic, the social and cultural impact was also vast. The social fabric of communities bound together by a particular industry or company weakened. Competition for scarce resources, as opposed to solidarity, has since become the norm.

Immigration to Britain, whilst in fact proving an economic boon, has given rise to the perception that there is even more competition for even scarcer resources. As we have already seen, many across the political divide have become concerned by the demographic changes brought about by immigration following the Second World War, which appeared to be speeding up in the twenty-first century, as net immigration began to rise substantially. When one considers the EU referendum in this context, the idea that optimism and confidence in the political establishment – blamed by millions for the decline of their town or city – would triumph, as they had done in Scotland and during the 2015 general election, appears fanciful and deeply naïve. Those who felt they had lost out as Britain transformed itself into a multicultural, post-industrial society – that sector of the population often referred to as the 'left behind' – had their say, and dealt a devastating blow to the status quo.

The north-east town of Hartlepool developed during the industrial revolution as a port through which to export coal. Heavy industry would come to dominate the town, and it developed a thriving shipbuilding and metal manufacturing sector, which enabled the town to grow. Its shipyards fell into terminal decline after the Second World War, and were soon followed by the steel industry. Deprivation and unemployment followed and Hartlepool is now one of the ten most deprived local authorities in the country.[3] During the EU referendum, just under 70 per cent of those voting chose to leave.

Christopher Akers-Belcher, leader of Hartlepool Council, told me in January 2017 that the vote to leave was heavily bound up with a sense that Hartlepool was being ignored and 'left behind'. Akers-Belcher, who was not surprised by the high Leave vote in the town, said that the MPs' expenses scandal of 2009 had lived long in the memory of the townspeople, crystallising a sense of mistrust which was to be compounded by the Coalition government's spending cuts from 2010: 'The MPs' expenses scandal is still current because people don't trust politics and they saw Leave as a real anti-establishment vote – it was a kickback against politics.' He went on to say, 'We have been disproportionately hit with funding cuts from what was a Tory Coalition government, to the government now. We've lost 50 per cent of our funding, so people have been hurt by that, and really, it was pushed forward by the Conservative government to have the referendum. Well, if you look at all referendums worldwide – people like to vote No. In any referendum, it doesn't matter what the outcome is, people like to vote against what they currently have.[4]

The South Yorkshire town of Barnsley voted over 68 per cent to leave in June 2016. Economic decline had set in from the late 1970s as the coal industry upon which the town depended dwindled before closing down, having become increasingly unprofitable and expensive for the government. Tens of thousands of the local population were employed in mining and complementary industries, and the town has simply not recovered. As the 'Experience Barnsley' museum puts it: 'The closure of the last collieries in the 1990s made many people redundant. Entire villages came out to watch the headgears tumble and the passing of a way of life they had known for generations.'

Dan Jarvis, Labour MP for Barnsley Central, told me that the vote to leave was overwhelmingly a revolt against an establishment blamed for closing down the pits and perceived as responsible for the town's degeneration and decline, coupled with larger national events such as the financial crisis and the expenses scandal. Many people in Barnsley, he said, 'think themselves, their families and Barnsley have been forgotten, have been left behind and have been ignored by a political establishment that either doesn't understand their concerns or the challenges they face or even worse, does understand them but either doesn't care or looks down upon them.' He went on, 'Brexit and the EU referendum brought all those concerns together. I have no doubt that a very significant number of people, locally, nationally as well, voted to leave the EU not having a specific critique of the EU themselves in their mind, but seeing it as the best opportunity they had ever had to express their concern and their dissatisfaction with a political establishment that they felt had not served them well for too long. And this was their moment to kick back against that and they took it.'[5]

Jarvis's Labour colleague in Great Grimsby, Melanie Onn MP, similarly argued that the high leave vote of just under 70 per cent was guided by the perception of the area's decline and a feeling that people weren't being listened to. Grimsby's North Sea fishing industry was once recognised as one of the largest and most dynamic in the world. It fell into terminal decline after the Second World War. The 'cod wars' of the 1970s, where Britain fought Iceland (and lost) over North Sea fishing rights further compounded its demise. A way of life was subsequently wiped out, and Grimsby, a town almost wholly geared to the fishing industry, has been unable to replace it with anything sustainable.

Onn told me that 'for the last forty years people have felt that they have not been getting a good deal out of the country, that increasingly it [Grimsby] has been left behind and over the last six years feeling the pressure [following the austerity policies of the Coalition government], even more so.' Many were 'very raw still that what was once a great fishing port is now no longer known for being great . . . it was an easy hook to hang a leave vote on despite there being a whole plethora of reasons.' Ultimately, 'People were crying out for change, the status quo was not meeting their needs, their expectations.'[6]

For many, the government's attitude to immigration was typical of an out-of-touch elite, despite the fact that most of the areas which voted in highest numbers to leave had experienced relatively little immigration. Even in Hartlepool, which has a foreign-born population of less than 3 per cent (in contrast to London, with an immigrant population recorded as 41 per cent in 2015), the locals were complaining of immigration to local politicians. Akers-Belcher told me, 'If somebody mentions immigration I would normally say to them "Could you just let me know how it has impacted on you?" And they'll quite openly say, "Well, it hasn't", and they will refer to what's in the press rather than the real-life impact on them in a community.' A certain element of local politicians had also been stoking fear of immigration during the referendum: 'I do think that some of the information being put out, particularly by Ukip, was a threat that you might not be affected now but immigration *will* come.'[7]

A prominent local Labour politician in the small West Yorkshire city of Wakefield, another former industrial area which voted over 66 per cent to leave, argued that the city's growing distrust of politicians was compounded by their approach to immigration policy. Wakefield has experienced EU migration first hand, and now has a 10,000-strong Polish community. Referring to the expenses scandal, he told me, 'No doubt that for the last eight years or so, there has been a huge shift in people's attitudes towards politicians, in particular national politicians, in particular a sense that "they are screwing us".'

Reflecting on the growth of concerns around immigration and distrust of politicians, he said 'A perfect storm was created.' He criticised David Cameron in particular for making promises on immigration that he couldn't keep, which only inflamed the public's suspicion of the political elite: 'What they say to folk is "Yeah, we hear your concerns. We're so concerned with what you're saying, we'll cut immigration" and they never do. That alienates people and there is some scapegoating [of immigrants] because of it and also it increases that distrust in politicians. Given the opportunity to put two fingers up at politicians and to sort out what they perceive as an immigration issue once and for all – they took it.'

Whilst Wakefield has seen significant migration from eastern Europe, its foreign-born population remains at 8 per cent – below the national average of just under 14 per cent. He nevertheless argued that people's trust in politicians has eroded over the issue of local immigration: 'All you need to look at are the promises made by Cameron, who said "we will reduce immigration to the tens of thousands" and people think "I'm being listened to" and then they see the figures year on year which have rocketed up. So anyone who says to me "we feel as though we're being listened to" must be crazy, they're clearly not being listened to, because they've gone up.'[8]

MPs in areas with low levels of immigration, such as Barnsley (5 per cent foreign-born population) and Grimsby (also 5 per cent), spoke of the regularity with which constituents brought up immigration, even though it was below half the national average in these areas. Dan Jarvis told me that in spite of Barnsley's low level of immigration, 'People's concerns about immigration as an issue are very high. So when you go out to talk to people as I do on a very regular basis, they will get to concerns about immigration pretty much before anything else.' Rather than other issues brought up by constituents such as declining public services and the NHS, for Jarvis, 'Immigration has been raised with me most commonly for a number of years before the referendum. It was the reason that was most regularly cited as the justification for voting to leave.'[9]

Melanie Onn argued similarly in Grimsby, stating that media portrayals of immigration had generated 'a lot of fear, a lot of unnecessary fear'. The financial crisis had also exacerbated people's negative perceptions of immigrants. Following the downturn, 'Invariably, people were worried about the number of jobs that were available, they were worried about declining wages and they were worried about "fitting everybody in". "There's not enough space" was a refrain frequently thrown back at me – "we are only a small island and we've run out of space".' Onn also believed that there was a widespread misconception in Grimsby that immigration was a subject which was not discussed by the political elite. She said, 'During the referendum campaign . . . people wanted to talk about immigration. People said Labour don't talk about immigration – *all* I talked about was immigration!'[10]

Even from this brief snapshot, it is not difficult to see how the growing contempt for politicians, coupled with fears over immigration and pessimism over the future, has changed the political landscape in Britain. In Rotherham, I spoke to two Ukip councillors in order to gain a sense of why the public was revolting against traditional politics. Rotherham grew from a small market town into a substantial coal mining and steel manufacturing centre. Its population rapidly expanded throughout the nineteenth and twentieth centuries as job opportunities abounded, employing men in their thousands. Since the collapse of the coal and steel industries, which began in the 1970s, Rotherham's economy had been particularly vulnerable and focused on industries highly prone to shocks, such as construction. In 2010, Rotherham had the fifteenth highest business insolvency rate in the country, according to a report by Experian.[11]

Yet the principal concerns of Ukip councillors Allen Cowles and Paul Hague related to immigration to the area. Rotherham in fact has a foreign-born population of just 3 per cent. The 2011 census showed it was nearly 94 per cent white, with a Pakistani community of around 3 per cent. Whilst its ethnic minority population doubled from 4 per cent to 8 per cent between 2001 and 2011, it is still well below the national average of 20 per cent. It voted just under 68 per cent to leave the EU in June 2016.

Allen Cowles, elected as a Ukip councillor in 2014, told me: 'We don't need waiters and people to make our beds and gardeners and all the rest of the jobs that the low paid do, nannies and the people who walk dogs and whatever, because we can't afford it. We don't have that kind of money in this part of the world. We are competing against those people who are coming and taking those low-end jobs and are then taking housing, which is in scarce supply around here, and taking schools and taking NHS resources, etc. It is not surprising that this part of the world voted the way it did.'

Cowles' principal concern was the Roma community which had been arriving from Romania since 2007, and who had already acquired a negative image amongst locals. He offered to show me around the town's Eastwood ward, where most of the Roma lived: 'We'll show you what the problems are having these people and not integrating them and simply allowing them to come here and do what the hell they want,' he said, banging his fist on the table. Cowles went on, 'I'm not a politician. I came into politics simply because I was fed up with what was happening in this town. I would have been a member of any party that opposed Labour. When Labour tell you they support the working man – that's the last thing that they do.'[12]

Cowles' colleague Paul Hague, also elected in 2014, was similarly angry about immigration in Rotherham: 'You don't have to be a rocket scientist to realise that if you put a significant number of a certain ethnicity into one area, they're going to stick together. They're not going to try and integrate.' Hague placed the blame for immigration at the door of the political establishment: 'A lot of people [in Rotherham] look at the people in power, the Conservative Party and especially the Labour Party and they look upon what they've done with open borders. They've tried to, in a way, ethnically cleanse their own country by allowing so many foreigners to come in.' He claimed that 'Tony Blair openly speaks, as he has in the past, that he basically signed up to allow Romanians to come in and Bulgarians and Polish, basically to increase their pool of voters and to give the middle finger to the Conservative Party by allowing all these people in.'

Hague framed the problems of immigration as economic, directly linking the referendum result to government immigration policy: 'If you will allow a whole flood of cheap labour into the country the existing workforce wages are not going to rise, and those people are going to eventually come to realise that and they're going to point the finger back at these people and say "why did you allow this?" and there should be a price to pay. The price to pay was on 23 June.'[13]

The traditionally quiet market town of Boston, Lincolnshire differs in many respects from former industrial towns in the north which voted so highly to leave the EU. Boston represented the highest leave vote in the whole country – just short of 76 per cent. Since the accession of the A8 countries to the EU in 2004, migration to Boston from East-Central Europe has swelled the town, most of the arrivals having come to work in its vast fruit and vegetable picking and food manufacturing sectors.

In ten years between 2001 and 2011, the population of Boston rose from 55,750 to 64,600 – and local authorities believe the figure to be much higher.[14] Over a quarter of Boston's inhabitants are now foreign-born, with the vast majority coming from A8 countries. The town has obtained national notoriety for its large migrant population, especially after a particularly unflattering article by Peter Hitchens in the *Daily Mail* in 2011. Hitchens, referring to the town as 'Boston, Lincolngrad', stated that the town had been 'upset, alarmed and riven by mass immigration in its hardest and most uncompromising form'.[15]

Peter Bedford, leader of Boston Council, believed that immigration played a prominent factor in the town's decision to vote overwhelmingly to leave the EU. He placed a large amount of the blame on the sensationalist media reporting exemplified by Hitchens: 'In Boston, a lot of people got the idea that if they voted out, to mean out, the migrants would disappear. Literally. Which of course was never, ever going to happen.' Bedford was however candid about the challenges immigration had brought to Boston, including downward pressure on wages and higher rents: 'If 20 to 25 per cent extra population, without any extra housing, descend on you in a four-year period – then you have got major problems.'[16]

Issues are far from exclusively economic. One noticeable feature of Boston is overhearing foreign languages, largely Polish, spoken in the town centre and shops. Michael Brookes, deputy leader of Boston Council, told me: 'Locals, walking around in their own town, start to feel uncomfortable, feeling like they are in a totally different place.'[17] Economic migration to Boston, which has unquestionably benefited the town, is rarely criticised from an economic point of view. But migration has had a significant cultural impact.

Boston's Tory MP Matt Warman, a Remainer elected in 2015, argued that the town's issues were largely down to the social impact brought about by rapid population change. They differed from those in the majority of leave areas which had experienced trivial numbers of migrants. He told me: 'If you say to people, "why do you think immigration is bad?" then they will say, I don't like the fact that you don't hear English voices on the streets as much as you used to, I don't like the changes in the high street, I don't like the anti-social behaviour. All of those – even if they are an unfair reflection of the communities which they are talking about – are very much taken from the lived experience [as opposed to media portrayals].'[18]

Great Yarmouth voted 71.5 per cent to leave in the EU

referendum. The coastal town in Norfolk has long been a popular tourist destination and also used to have a thriving herring-
fishing industry. Fishing began to decline after the Second
World War and the advent of cheap package holidays to the
European continent has significantly damaged tourism. During
the 1970s, Great Yarmouth saw nine million tourist nights; by
2014, this had nearly halved to under five million. The town nevertheless remains highly dependent on tourism and just under
80 per cent of jobs are service-based.[19] The seasonal nature of
work in Great Yarmouth means a high influx of workers from
outside, and the town has seen migration from East-Central
Europe – with around 10 per cent of the town's population born
outside the country.

Great Yarmouth Council leader, Graham Plant, argued that
immigration had greatly contributed to the area's significant
leave vote. 'We have had a huge influx in Great Yarmouth –
10,000 within five years prior to the vote. It created a populist
movement of whether we did want so many people coming from
Europe, not only into the country, but into this area.' He argued
that over the past few years there had been a widespread feeling
that 'jobs were always going to immigrants, houses were going
to immigrants, all the problems of the NHS were down to immigrants. All the problems in the country were being attributed
to immigrants . . . If you can get a populist movement behind
that, which unfortunately they did, people's thoughts were: we
should be out [of the EU].'

Given that Great Yarmouth is one of the poorest areas of
the country, he continued: 'When you get deprivation you get
people who have needs and they expect the government to help
them. If they see that help going to a new element, which in
this case would be immigration, what they say is "instead of me

getting a council house, you're giving it to a foreigner. Instead of me getting a doctor's surgery appointment, you're giving it to a foreigner."'

Plant had experienced the powerful anti-establishment rhetoric of Ukip prior to the referendum. In 2014, ten Ukip councillors were elected to Great Yarmouth Council, leading to a hung administration. 'There was a really serious anti-establishment rhetoric going on in Yarmouth. Nigel Farage was pushing all the time the idea that "it's the establishment that's causing all these problems and they're only looking after themselves, they're not looking after you, the people".' Plant recognised the political potency of such rhetoric: 'It's a powerful message to send out to this town. You've got to remember that Great Yarmouth is probably the sixth most deprived area in the country and the most deprived area in the East of England.'[20]

Lowestoft in east Suffolk, just down the road from Great Yarmouth, is another coastal town on the east coast which has seen significant decline. Fleets of fishing trawlers regularly used to leave the town's port, but that has all but ceased. The Eastern Coach Works used to be a large employer before it was closed in 1987, as did shipbuilding firm Brooke Marine, which was wound up in 1992. Waveney district, of which Lowestoft forms a major part, voted just shy of 63 per cent to leave in the EU referendum.

Peter Aldous, Conservative MP for Waveney, who campaigned for Remain, told me that the high leave vote 'didn't come as a surprise if you had looked at previous elections and the reaction I got on the doorstep'. He attributed the vote to local anger over the decline of Lowestoft and similar towns: 'In a lot of these coastal communities, the economies have performed very badly over the past thirty or forty years. Britain traditionally was a trading nation, places like Lowestoft, with the fishing industry, traded globally and what they did was at the forefront of Britain's wealth and position in the world in the past. And if you look in Lowestoft, it was the very model of a seaside, coastal economy, in terms of the fishing, the shipbuilding related to that, television factory, a coachworks, it had a good industrial base which over a period of thirty or forty years has declined dramatically.'

Long-term decline in Lowestoft was compounded by the 2008 financial crisis, according to Aldous: 'The recession of the late noughties was a particularly deep recession. We have, if you look at a macro level, recovered from that.' Nevertheless, there was a significant group of people on low incomes 'who have not had the benefits of that improvement in economic conditions. Who feel left behind. I feel that was the issue they were getting out at the [EU referendum] vote last year. From my perspective, we've got to recognise the concerns that those people were sending out to people like us.'[21]

Bert Poole, a Ukip county councillor from Lowestoft, is old enough to remember what Lowestoft used to be like in its heyday. 'My wife was the general secretary of Brooke Marine – they built high spec patrol vessels and gunboats, that was shut.' Yet it was immigration that began to provide votes for Ukip in the area: 'When I was canvassing for county council elections, all people were saying was "I'm going to vote Ukip because I can't stand all this immigration". So they were driving us, we weren't driving them. We were filling a need.'

Lowestoft's migrant community is in fact very small – around 4 per cent of the population is foreign-born. According to Poole, the town had been 'used as a dumping ground for asylum seekers and social misfits from the inner cities who went to Lowestoft and other seaside towns'. He argues that this 'caused a bit of friction. All the livelihoods of people had gone; all the high skilled jobs had gone. And now you're just bringing in all this cheap unskilled labour.'[22]

Further south, on the Essex–Suffolk border, Clacton-on-Sea voted just shy of 70 per cent to leave the EU.[23] Clacton used to be a substantial tourist destination – the second Butlin's holiday camp was built there in 1938 and closed in 1983. Like other British seaside towns, cheap package holidays to sunnier destinations on the continent have contributed to its decline. In 2010, the Office for National Statistics found that Clacton was the second most deprived seaside town in the country. The village of Jaywick, a suburb of Clacton, was still ranked ingloriously as the most deprived neighbourhood in the whole of England.

Politically, the town came to attention in 2014 as its Conservative Member of Parliament, Douglas Carswell, defected to Ukip and triggered a by-election, which he convincingly won – making him Ukip's first elected Member of Parliament.[24] Prior to the by-election in October 2014, *The Times* columnist Matthew Parris poured scorn on the town, stating that the 'Tories should turn their backs on Clacton': 'Understand that Clacton-on-Sea is going nowhere. Its voters are going nowhere, it's rather sad, and there's nothing more to say. This is Britain on crutches. This is tracksuit-and-trainers Britain, tattoo-parlour Britain, all-our-yesterdays Britain.'[25]

When I discussed the leave vote with Carswell, who helped to found the Vote Leave campaign, he bemoaned the fact that both the Conservative and Labour parties liked to talk tough on immigration without ever intending to do anything about it: 'When I was a Tory I used to notice that round about the party conference season, David Blunkett would issue some tough headline on immigration. I used to sit in the Tory Research

Department at the time and we used to say, "it's coming up to party conference season, they're going to say something tough on immigration, what can we say that's tough on immigration?" It's like the Soviet system where officials issue press releases on tractor production targets and it has no relation at all to what's happening in the real world. And that's the problem. It undermines the whole currency of politics.'

Carswell holds what he refers to as 'elites' in particular contempt and claims that their failure to understand the public and provide services led to the Brexit revolt. Speaking of the establishment and the likes of Parris, he told me: 'Like 100 years ago, the Romanovs would have been sitting in their Winter Palace and not aware of what was coming. Our elites today, like the Romanovs, are oblivious to the changes that are happening. But it doesn't mean that it's not happening.'

Carswell argued that constituents in Clacton, like many others in the country, viewed Brexit as part of a revolt against poor public administration dominated by an incompetent elite, of which immigration was just one element: 'Often when people say they are concerned about immigration, it's not hostility towards outsiders, it is a shorthand way of talking about a loss of control. That's why the referendum campaign slogan we used about taking back control was so powerful.' According to Carswell, 'People feel a deep-seated contempt for the way in which decision making in their countries, which are supposed to be democracies, is made by unofficial institutions, of which the supranational institutions are the epitome.' He rejected the idea that the revolt against the established political order was due to parochial nationalism: 'It's a dissatisfaction with the crapness of public administration in this country. Before we had Netflix, before we had supermarkets which were prepared to come and deliver groceries when you wanted them to, before we had banks that you could log into on a Saturday afternoon, people put up with that appalling level of public administration. But they're not putting up with it now. This is what is fuelling the insurgency in the western world, it's a technologically driven thing. It is not a nativist driven thing.'

Ultimately, he blamed rising public concern over immigration on inaction by the elites he referred to, which had created a vacuum filled by inflammatory tabloid headlines. The mainstream media, he said, 'have for years been neglectful of what is a legitimate issue of public policy debate'. Furthermore, there was 'A lack of honesty on the part of sensible, intelligent home secretaries over the years, promising people something they can't deliver, making things that sound tough, but have little consequence in the real world. All of this creates an appetite of frustration for people to buy a newspaper that says stuff that it shouldn't really be saying. People complain about the shrillness of some of the tabloid headlines, but that is a direct consequence of the stupidity and lack of action by successive home secretaries.'[26]

David Cameron complained during his campaign to become Prime Minister in 2010 that Britain was dominated by 'an elite who thinks it knows best'. He argued that 'people have lost control' and 'the politicians have forgotten, the public are the master, we are the servant'. He pledged to 'blow apart the old system', something which would indeed occur during his premiership, though in a very different way from how he had envisaged.[27] By pledging the Conservative Party to a European referendum, Cameron was offering a referendum on the political establishment, and on immigration.

Given the increasing mistrust in politicians, particularly over their handling of rising immigration levels, the public's decision appears less shocking and more explicable. Dissatisfaction with British politics and what Britain had become was widespread, particularly in northern industrial and seaside towns. But rather than being restricted to Britain, the phenomenon was and is in fact engulfing the western world.

8
A WESTERN DISEASE

*Financial globalisation and Islamist globalisation are helping each
other out. Those two ideologies want to bring France to its knees.*

Marine Le Pen, launch of presidential campaign,
Sunday 5 February 2017

Having looked at the climate in Britain, which has seen a rise in
popular sentiment deeply hostile to political elites, moving our
focus to western Europe and indeed the USA we can begin to
see how Brexit is indicative of a wider revolt against 'politics as
usual', particularly over the issue of immigration.

Many of the same trends which saw Britain vote for Brexit
also saw Donald Trump win the United States presidential election in November 2016. The make-up of support for Ukip and
the BNP bears close resemblance to that of the Front National
in France or the Dutch Party for Freedom. Ultimately, to look at
Britain in isolation would be to decontextualise it from a much
wider trend which is engulfing the West. What occurred in
2016, which saw both Brexit and Trump's election, was nothing short of a political earthquake. Trump's success marked the
biggest achievement for the radical right in the West. By taking
the presidency of the most powerful country in the world, he
could have a legitimising effect on the radical right in Europe
and beyond.

Much as in Britain, explanations of the right-wing revolt across the West as a cultural, rather than a purely economic one are the most convincing. Whilst we have already seen that high votes for Brexit were delivered in areas which had experienced profound economic decline, Professor Eric Kaufmann argues that the growth of the radical right is 'mainly about the question of immigration and ethnic transformation'.

Kaufmann is critical of economic arguments which seek to explain the rise of right-wing populism across the West. 'It's very hard when you live through this to see that economics is not the driver. You see an area which maybe voted more heavily for Brexit and it might look a bit more rundown, and you might make that association, but it's not the most important association.' Furthermore, 'If you look at the individual survey data you don't see income being that important. In Britain it is true that if you are lower income or lower skilled you are somewhat more likely to have voted Leave. But in the US, in terms of the Trump vote, it's totally not an issue. Even in Britain it is much less of an issue than education levels. No qualifications vs a degree, for example, is much more important than rich vs poor.'

Kaufmann tells me that 'the material argument really doesn't hold water. There's two key questions: why the populist right and not the populist left? If it's really about annoyance at elites, why has the trend in the West been towards the populist right more than the populist left?' He argues that if you 'compare the recession with the migrant crisis and look at their effects on populist right support and on what people think are the most important issues', the recession had zero effect except in southern Europe, while 'the migrant crisis had an enormous effect'. Another comparison Kaufmann makes is that supporters of radical left-wing Labour leader Jeremy Corbyn 'are typically not that well off but they have degrees. Similarly, someone who is a successful plumbing contractor or someone who has done well who doesn't have any qualifications would be a very strong candidate for voting Brexit. It's not about material circumstances.'

Kaufmann goes on: 'I can see why other people are making the economic argument. In a way if you want to have hope for the future then you think "well, we can pull a few familiar economic levers and that will cure the problem" but I don't think that is going to work.' Ultimately, 'Demographic change, immigration and identity threat are all linked, because you have got a rising share of the populations of these countries that are foreign born and of a different ethnic background to the majority.' He argues, 'You have got a demographic shift that is altering people's environment and challenging their identity. Ethnic national identity is about the association between the nation – the territorial political unit – and the ethnic group, which is to do with ancestry, culture, religion and colour, etc. There is an increasing disjuncture between the nation state and the ethnic majority feel it's losing its grip on that.'[1]

Multicultural Europe

The beginnings of the right-wing backlash in Europe are closely linked to the changes which occurred in migration patterns following the Second World War. As a result of these an unprecedented demographic shift occurred in the ethnic composition of Europe which has continued to speed up. Prior to that, much global migration had been from Europe outwards, most often to the imperial possessions of colonial powers such as France, the Netherlands and Portugal. Following decolonisation in the 1950s and 60s, western Europe experienced a new wave of migration from both southern Europe and outside the continent. France in particular saw hundreds of thousands arrive from North Africa, including many from Algeria, following the bloody French-Algerian war which raged between 1954 and 1962.

The majority of migration was the result of bilateral agreements made between West European countries (largely France, West Germany, Belgium, the Netherlands and Luxembourg) which imported 'guest workers' (known in Germany as *Gastarbeiter*) and other European countries such as Italy, Spain, Greece and Portugal, as well as predominantly Muslim countries on Europe's periphery like Turkey, Tunisia and Morocco. Similarly, France made agreements with Senegal, Mali and the Ivory Coast. By the late 1960s, over a million *Gastarbeiter* had arrived in West Germany alone and hundreds of thousands of new workers were arriving in the country each year.

The arrival of guest workers meant the development of thriving ethnic communities in western Europe. The number of foreign workers in Germany grew from 280,000 in 1960 to nearly 2.6 million in 1973. By 1974, Germany had an immigrant population of 4.1 million, in contrast to 690,000 in 1960. The arrival of guest workers transformed the demographics of western European countries from predominantly white communities into multicultural and multiracial ones. The Turkish community in Germany, which originates from the guest worker programme, is now over five million strong. France has a similarly sized community of Algerians. In the Netherlands, nearly 400,000 Moroccans live in the country, the majority of whom arrived as guest workers.

Unlike migrants to Britain from the Commonwealth who arrived in the 1940s and 50s, guest workers were not citizens and were officially only temporary residents there for the purposes of employment. They provided affordable labour for businesses within the setting of economies booming as a result of, among other factors, European integration. As governments imposed limits on guest worker programmes in a bid to curb immigration in the 1970s, few workers returned home and immigration actually remained steady or increased as their families joined them. Governments expected and even encouraged guest workers to go home, but the majority had created lives for themselves in their host country and did not want to leave.

In the late 1970s and 1980s, political disenchantment grew in western Europe. There was public pessimism over the future as economies began to deindustrialise, as well as anxiety over the changing nature of societies, which had come about following the admission of guest workers. Many simply began to disengage from politics. In the first unified German election in 1990, 10 million did not vote and turnout was at under 78 per cent, in contrast to 90.7 per cent in 1976. Many were drawn to populist, radical right-wing parties who sought to exploit public anxiety over immigration and fears over unemployment and the crime which came with it. Anger was also stoked by the rise in applications for asylum in western Europe in the 1980s and 1990s, which increased from around 70,000 in the mid-1980s to nearly 320,000 in the early 1990s. Radical right-wing parties sought to exploit this, as well as the growing visibility of non-white men, women and children in towns and cities.

Populations appeared more concerned with migrants from outside Europe than those from within. In a 1990 poll in France, over 50 per cent of respondents claimed there were too many North African immigrants in France, and over a third said the same about migrants from sub-Saharan Africa, whereas only 13 per cent believed there were too many migrants from Spain.[2] Immigration was ranked as the second most important issue in France in 1992, with only unemployment ranking higher. In a poll conducted the same year in Germany, only 23 per cent of respondents said they were in favour of a multicultural society.

The growth of the radical right can ultimately be seen as a backlash against the demographic change which has been witnessed in western Europe since the 1950s – change which has only sped up in the twenty-first century. By 2012, Germany had a foreign-born population of nearly 11 million. France's foreign-born population made up 12 per cent of the country in 2013, Sweden's stood at 16 per cent. The largest in Europe was Switzerland, which had a foreign-born population of just under 30 per cent in 2013. The UK's foreign-born population in late 2015 stood at around 9 million, just over 13 per cent of the population.

Fascist echoes in western Europe

The radical right is, clearly, not a recent phenomenon. Many surging far right parties have their roots within the interwar fascist tradition. Others, such as the Front National in France, were founded in the 1970s and had begun to achieve success and influence mainstream politics by the 1980s. There has certainly been a very recent rise in support for these parties across Europe, and whilst the populist surge has only recently become apparent to many, xenophobic and populist politics have a rich history. Nor are these movements simply minor parties on the fringes, as perhaps they once were. Austria had a far right party in government in 2000. The Swiss People's Party has won national elections. Many others, as in Denmark and the Netherlands, have propped up minority governments. A number have finished second in national elections, achieving substantial parliamentary representation. Ultimately, populism poses the greatest challenge to liberal democracy in Europe and the United States since the Second World War. It has been growing for some time and that growth has become turbocharged over the past two years.

To understand the beginnings of contemporary populism, which has become the norm in most western countries, we must turn to France. During the 1950s, a populist, anti-establishment movement on the right arose in the form of Pierre Poujade's French Union and Fraternity, also known as the Poujadist movement. The anti-Semitic Poujade had fascist sympathies during the interwar period and was dubbed 'Poujadolf' by left-wing opponents. Relying on his own exceptional charisma, he made direct appeals to people for revolution, pledging to kick out the 'old gang'. His party won just under 13 per cent of the vote in the 1956 legislative elections, yet support began to wane shortly after splits within his ideologically diffuse movement became obvious. The Poujadist movement was relatively minor and short-lived, but it demonstrated briefly the success of xenophobic populism, which chastised elites and the establishment. One man elected in 1956 for the Poujadists – Jean-Marie Le Pen – would take radical right-wing populism to a new level in the 1980s.

Le Pen, who fought in the French-Algerian War (and has long faced allegations of engaging in torture during his service), would found the Front National (FN) in 1972. The party was initially a rabble of former veterans of the Algerian war, people involved in the collaborationist wartime Vichy government, neo-Nazis and Catholic traditionalists who hated the French Republic and longed for the restoration of monarchy. For a decade, the FN was completely marginal to French politics and the party frequently polled below 1 per cent of the vote.

Aurélien Mondon argues that it took 'some time for the far right, after the Second World War, to accept that the old paradigm wasn't working anymore, that the old biological racism [of the fascist era] couldn't be brought back'. Organisations had to adapt to the postwar political culture and at least pay lip service to ideas of tolerance and diversity. In France, at the beginning of the Front National in the 1970s, it was 'an openly neo-fascist movement who believed in white supremacy'. When this clearly wasn't going to work, it 'needed them to change their tack on certain issues. The whole idea of difference was no longer "we are superior to you [non-whites]" but "we are all equal, diversity is amazing, but we need to protect diversity by you staying where you're from and I will stay where I'm from".'

The far right had 'consciously moved away from racial superiority to the idea of cultural incompatibility, which at the end of the day is exactly the same kind of racism. It still says "your culture is innately different from mine and we cannot mix". It allowed them to say "it's not me being superior, we are just different".'[3] This change of strategy would contribute to the electoral rise of the FN and act as a guide for many other far right parties across Europe. Following the election of Socialist François Mitterrand in 1981 and a decline in support for the mainstream Gaullist right, the FN's fortunes began to dramatically improve.

Le Pen's criticism of immigration began to cut through and he established himself as an extremely competent and charismatic media performer. In 1984, the party won just under 11 per cent in the European Parliament elections and Le Pen was elected to a chamber in which he still sits. A further electoral breakthrough would be made in 1986. The embattled President Mitterrand had deviously changed the parliamentary electoral system to one of proportional representation, and was suspected of doing so to use the FN to weaken the mainstream right. The FN won just shy of 10 per cent of the vote and was rewarded with thirty-five deputies. Le Pen was winning over a substantial number of right-wing voters but was also successful in areas of Paris with high immigrant populations.

The party's support would plateau at around 10 to 15 per cent for the next decade at least, but its steady support was reflective of a growing number of parties in Europe who sought to use populist and anti-establishment xenophobia to win votes. Many, like the FN, had their origins within fascism and the right-wing extremist movements of the interwar period. Increasingly they sought to mask this fanatical core with more palatable rhetoric about 'freedom' and 'democracy'. Tirades against an almost mythical establishment obscured deeply sinister ideas on race and immigration.

The radical right began to succeed in other countries in Europe, following in Le Pen's footsteps. One early example of a successful radical right-wing populist party comes from Austria. The Freedom Party of Austria (FPÖ) was founded in 1956 and led by a former Nazi SS officer. Whilst the party had several political guises, Jörg Haider would transform it into an electorally successful, radical right-wing populist movement when he became leader in 1986. Vigorously opposed to immigration and multiculturalism, Haider promoted a nativist agenda which pledged 'Austria First'. The flamboyant and charming leader would begin to criticise the European Union and the 'establishment' in a manner common to many parties today.

Haider was elected Governor of Carinthia in 1989, although his first stint in the position would be short-lived. He caused controversy with a number of inflammatory statements; praising the 'orderly' employment policies of the Third Reich in 1991, he was forced to step down. His greatest triumph came in the parliamentary elections of 2000 where the FPÖ finished second, achieving 27 per cent of the vote. The party subsequently entered a right-wing coalition with the mainstream conservative Austrian People's Party, although Haider was excluded. The international community was horrified by the coalition, the EU imposing diplomatic sanctions on one of its own member states.

The FPÖ's electoral success was an early sign that the fascist origins of many parties were becoming less of a concern as the war generation began to decline. The conservative chancellor who entered into the coalition, Wolfgang Schüssel, pledged to 'tame the beast' – a strategy similarly employed by the conservative Weimar elites who had entered into a coalition with Adolf Hitler in 1933. The party, unable to impose much of its radical programme, split in 2005, but its experience in government by no means tainted its image as anti-establishment, and it remains a major force in Austrian politics to this day.

Another worrying development, one which stunned the world and is highly indicative of the threat posed by the far right to more mainstream parties, came in the 2002 French presidential election. Jean-Marie Le Pen, who had now been active in far right and populist politics for over half a century, achieved over 4.8 million votes – just under 200,000 more than Socialist candidate Lionel Jospin – ensuring second place in the first round of voting. This meant that Le Pen would face President Jacques

Chirac in the final round, providing him with a previously unthinkable national platform. Voters were appalled by the choice between the deeply unpopular President Chirac – who had been accused of financial fraud – and a man who could easily be described as a neo-fascist. Left-wing voters were nevertheless urged to 'vote for the crook, not the fascist'.[4]

The contest was easily won by Chirac by a margin of over 60 per cent. But the fact that Le Pen, known for his inflammatory statements and extremism – in 1987 he referred to Nazi gas chambers as a mere 'detail of history' – could make it to the final round of the election was deeply alarming. It demonstrated rising levels of political disenchantment, particularly over immigration and demographic changes. Increasingly, the right-wing populist vote appeared to cut across traditional party lines, appealing to working-class as much as middle-class voters.

Right-wing populism began to grow in the Netherlands at around the same period in a country renowned among many for its relatively placid political debate. Islam began to become a prominent scapegoat of the radical right following the 9/11 attacks in the United States, and the growth in Islamophobia can be witnessed particularly sharply in the Netherlands. Pim Fortuyn rose to become the country's most notable populist in 2002, yet he differed in many respects from Haider and Le Pen.

Fortuyn focused on issues such as multiculturalism and had proposed a ban on Muslim immigration, yet he was openly gay and sought to present himself as the defender of the country's liberal tradition, which he alleged was under threat from immigration and Islam. He said in 2002, 'I don't hate Islam. I consider it a backward culture. I have travelled much in the world. And wherever Islam rules, it's just terrible.'[5] Fortuyn was assassinated during the 2002 national election campaign by an environmentalist who was angered by his rhetoric about Muslims. An electoral shock was still felt nine days after the murder, when his party, Pim Fortuyn List, finished second overall with 17 per cent of the vote.

Immigration and Islam have been a strong feature of Dutch politics ever since, particularly since the barbaric murder of Theo van Gogh. A film director responsible for the anti-Muslim film *Submission*, Van Gogh was cycling to work one morning when he was shot and stabbed to death by a Dutch-Moroccan Islamist. Radical right-wing populism in the Netherlands was soon to be defined by Geert Wilders, formerly of the mainstream conservative Party for Freedom and Democracy. Wilders founded the Party for Freedom in 2006.

Best identified by his bright blond bouffant, Wilders had continuously been critical of multiculturalism, but is particularly known for his hard-line stance on Islam. He once said 'Islam is not a religion, it's an ideology, the ideology of a retarded culture.' Describing the Koran, he stated: 'The Koran is a fascist book which incites violence. That is why this book, just like *Mein Kampf*, must be banned.'[6] He was himself banned from entering the UK in 2009 after being invited by Ukip leader Lord Pearson to show his anti-Islamic film *Fitna*, in which the classic anti-Muslim trope of linking all Muslims with the actions of terrorists was vividly exhibited.

Few areas in Europe appear immune to the radical right surge. Scandinavian countries, glorified by many as examples of liberal, tolerant societies with well-functioning social democratic governments, have seen right-wing populist parties rise significantly over the past two decades. The Sweden Democrats, founded in 1988, was a party based on the neo-Nazi tradition. It began to clean up its image in the late 1990s and adopted a more xenophobic and populist stance. For much of its existence, it polled at under 2 per cent. However, by 2010 it had achieved nearly 6 per cent of the vote. In 2014, this had more than doubled, to just short of 13 per cent.

Sweden's neighbours, Denmark, have seen the unprecedented rise of anti-immigrant populism in the shape of the Danish People's Party. The party blossomed much more quickly than the Sweden Democrats, and after winning 12.1 per cent in the 2001 elections, was already capable of significantly influencing the centre-right government's hard-line immigration policy. Following the 2005 cartoon scandal, where a series of images depicting the prophet Muhammad were published by Danish newspaper *Jyllands Posten*, causing outrage in the Muslim world and within Denmark's Muslim community, its support dramatically increased. In 2014, the party topped the Danish polls with nearly 27 per cent of the vote.

Norway has similarly witnessed the rise of radical right-wing populism. The Progress Party was founded in the early 1970s as a libertarian, free-market political party. It soon began to focus more on immigration and cultural issues in the 1990s and by 1997 it was already finishing second in national elections with over 15 per cent of the vote. By 2005 its support had increased to 22 per cent and continued to grow.

The support of the Progress Party plummeted after former member Anders Breivik carried out his brutal massacre at a left-wing summer camp in July 2011. However, in 2013, it joined in a governing coalition with the Conservative Party. In Finland, a radical right-wing populist party – the Finns Party – has similarly entered a coalition. The party, which achieved over 22 per cent of the vote in 2015, blends nationalism with left-wing economic policies and support for Finland's generous welfare state. Its charismatic and full-figured leader, Timo Soini, is currently the country's foreign minister.

Goodbye Communism, hello nationalism

The rise of the radical right is not limited to western or northern Europe and has engulfed the continent's former communist states. The biggest success has come in Hungary. In the late 1980s, as the country was breaking free from the shackles of communism, Victor Orban founded Fidesz (the Alliance of Young Democrats). The party would move from a relatively liberal position to one of nationalist conservatism, and had much in common with the populist radical right seen in the rest of Europe. After his first term as Prime Minister between 1998 and 2002, Orban was re-elected in 2010. Since then, he has transformed Hungary into what he himself calls an 'illiberal democracy', and what one could argue is the prototype state for most radical right populists across Europe. This has taken Hungary down an increasingly authoritarian path and has led to the centralisation of power, the weakening of institutions and restrictions on media freedom.

The past decade in Hungary has also seen the rise of an extreme right movement – Jobbik. The racist party has significant neo-Nazi elements and is also highly anti-Semitic. Jobbik, which boasts a paramilitary wing similar to the Nazi SA, achieved a staggering 20 per cent in the 2014 legislative election. When you add Jobbik's vote to the 45 per cent achieved by Orban in that election, you can witness the alarmingly high level of support for radical and extreme right parties in Hungary. As Joe Mulhall argues, there is a symbiotic relationship between Orban and Jobbik, with the former aping the latter: 'Jobbik don't need to take control of Hungary because Victor Orban, a supposedly mainstream politician, will say "Muslims are invading Europe"'– thereby normalising that kind of inflammatory language.'[7]

Such wide support for xenophobic groups has increased the normalisation of deeply intolerant attitudes to migrants, and in particular to the 300,000 strong Roma community both in Hungary and the wider region. This xenophobia and anti-Roma sentiment is by no means limited to Hungary, but has stained much of East-Central Europe. In Slovakia, anti-Roma billboards were erected by the far right Slovak National Party, which achieved over 12 per cent in the 2006 election, stating 'Let's not put up with parasites!' and 'How much longer are we going to pay for the Roma?' The party's former leader, Ján Slota, also attacked the nation's Hungarian community, in language reminiscent of the Third Reich, as 'the cancer of the Slovak nation . . . without delay we need to remove them from the body of the nation'.[8]

One country which has acted as a model for Orban, functioning as an ideological magnet for much of the radical right in Europe, is Vladimir Putin's Russia. Putin has been at the top of Russian politics since the economic crises of the 1990s and has increasingly consolidated power into his own hands. Previously independent – whilst admittedly dysfunctional and corrupt – institutions, including the national parliament (the Duma) have gradually become moulded in the interests of Putin and his United Russia Party. Political opponents have been silenced and prosecuted by means of trumped-up charges and Russia has introduced sinisterly intolerant laws against homosexuals and other minorities. Much like the Cold War Soviet bloc in many respects, Putin's Russia presents an alternative to western liberalism – conservative, insular, authoritarian and xenophobic, with a strongman at the head of a powerful government. As Russia's stock has risen on the world stage, the appeal of Putinism has grown, as indicated by the radical right's support for his annexation of Crimea in 2014 and his subsequent manoeuvres in Ukraine.

Far right ascendency

The far right began to achieve success as attitudes to immigration hardened across western Europe. We have already witnessed how negativity towards immigration in Britain began to grow in the first decade of the twenty-first century and beyond. Whilst concern over immigration was much higher generally in the UK than in Europe and the United States, a similar trend can be witnessed Europe-wide. In 2011, a poll conducted for Transatlantic Trends found increasingly hardening attitudes towards immigration in many European countries. When asked whether 'immigration is more of a problem than an opportunity' in 2008, 39 per cent in France agreed. In 2011, the figure had risen to 46 per cent; by 2014, it had reached 50 per cent.[9] In 2014, 64 per cent of French citizens disapproved of their government's handling of immigration, while 51 per cent were similarly dissatisfied in Germany and 57 per cent in the Netherlands. In the United States, a substantial 71 per cent disapproved.[10]

Another poll, conducted by Pew in 2014, found that attitudes to immigration were generally negative in Europe. In Greece and Italy (two countries where refugees have arrived in large numbers), 86 per cent and 80 per cent respectively desired less immigration. In France, the figure was a comfortable majority of 57 per cent. Even in Germany, where citizens were less pessimistic, a mere 14 per cent desired more immigration. Underlying these attitudes was the belief that migrants did not want to assimilate. In Germany 59 per cent held this view. In France it was 54 per cent, and a huge 77 per cent in Italy.[11] Polling has generally shown Europeans to be particularly sceptical of Muslim immigration. A poll in 2016, again conducted by Pew, unearthed increasingly negative views of Muslims. Pew Research found that 30 per cent of respondents in France viewed Muslims unfavourably, 29 per cent in Germany, 35 per cent in the Netherlands and a substantial 69 per cent in Italy.[12] Viewed within this context, we can now look at the rise of the radical right across Europe in more detail.

There were indications in the 2014 European elections that concern about immigration was working in the favour of anti-immigration populist movements. The Front National, led by Jean-Marie Le Pen's daughter Marine, who sought to moderate the party's image, finished first in France with just under 25 per cent of the vote. Over two million people in Germany voted for the brand-new radical right party, Alternative for Germany. Ukip won the most seats in the United Kingdom. The Danish People's Party finished first in Denmark, whilst the neo-Nazi, extreme right Golden Dawn in Greece finished third with over 9 per cent of the vote.

Whilst right-wing populism can be seen to have gathered impetus since the turn of the twenty-first century, 2015 could easily be regarded as a transformative year for the right across Europe. This was a year in which events appeared to fit their narrative and support began to seriously grow. It was the year the radical right truly appeared to break through and the idea of radical right governments began to appear conceivable. It began with the *Charlie Hebdo* attacks by French Muslim terrorists. The world was horrified by the brutal and widely publicised attack, prompting a large social media response: *Je suis Charlie*.

The attack was exploited by many as being demonstrative of the failure of multiculturalism and the danger of militant Islam. A regional leader of Alternative for Germany responded by saying, 'This bloodbath proves wrong those who laughed or ignored the fears of so many people about a looming danger of Islamism.' Geert Wilders announced in a video he posted online: 'This is not the end of the misery, but just the beginning. Our elites have saddled us with an enormous problem . . . no one can deny the truth any longer. It is Islam that inspires the murderers every time. It is Muhammad, the so-called prophet. It is the Koran. That is the problem and nothing else.'[13] Victor Orban responded shortly afterwards and related the attack to multiculturalism: 'We don't want to see significantly sized minorities with different cultural characteristics and backgrounds among us. We want to keep Hungary as Hungary.'[14]

Eclipsing the impact of terror attacks, Sarah de Lange argues that the refugee crisis was hugely important in terms of the recent rise in far right support, describing it as 'a catalyst that has pushed these parties from, in many cases 15 to 20 per cent to over 20 per cent'.[15] The refugee crisis in the summer of 2015 was a gift to the far right, as more than a million refugees from the Middle East and North Africa entered the European continent through Greece and Italy. The chaotic nature of this mass movement of people gave rise to the idea that the situation was completely out of control and images were conjured by the far right of 'the barbarians at the gate'. Angela Merkel's humanitarian decision to accept hundreds of thousands of refugees into Germany angered both the far right and numerous mainstream politicians – many of whom recognised the positive impact it could potentially have on far right fortunes. It would be Victor Orban, leading Hungary – through which many refugees had travelled – who would increasingly develop an image amongst the radical right of a strongman leading on the front line against the migrant 'invasion'.

Orban, who constructed a razor wire fence to keep migrants out, blamed Germany for the problem, and at a meeting of the European Council delivered a strong rebuke to Europe's elites who sought to provide sanctuary to refugees. He also wrote in German newspaper *Frankfurter Allgemeine Zeitung*:

> Everything which is now taking place before our eyes threatens to have explosive consequences for the whole of Europe... Those arriving have been raised in another religion, and represent a radically different culture. Most of them are not Christians, but Muslims. This is an important question, because Europe and European identity is rooted in Christianity... Is it not worrying in itself that European Christianity is now barely able to keep Europe Christian? There is no alternative, and we have no option but to defend our borders.[16]

Marine Le Pen, leader of the Front National, claimed the refugees were bogus, and were predominantly economic migrants trying to cheat the system for financial gain: 'I have seen images of the illegal immigrants coming... And of course, 99 per cent of these images are men.' She went on, 'I think that the men who flee their country and leave their family there, are not doing it to flee persecution. This is obviously done for economic reasons.'[17] When another Islamist attack hit Paris in November 2015, with several of the perpetrators having used the refugee route to re-enter the continent, refugees began to become synonymous with terrorism.

Negative attitudes to refugees found in the Pew Global Attitudes Survey conducted in 2016 provide part of the explanation for the rise in support for the radical right. In Hungary, 76 per cent believed admitting refugees increased the likelihood of terrorism, while 61 per cent believed the same in both Germany and the Netherlands. Seventy-three per cent in Poland saw refugees from Iraq and Syria as a 'major threat', as did 69 per cent in Greece and Hungary and 45 per cent in France. People were overwhelmingly critical of the EU's response to the refugee crisis. Eighty-eight per cent were critical in Sweden – a country which, as a proportion of its population, gave sanctuary to the most refugees. In Poland, 71 per cent were critical, in France 70 per cent and in Germany 67 per cent.[18]

The far right backlash in response to the refugee crisis was perhaps felt most sharply in Germany – the land of sanctuary for most fleeing war and persecution. In 2014 the country had already seen the rise of the Islamophobic street-based movement, Pegida, which drew thousands to its provocative street marches. Radical right party Alternative for Germany was only founded in 2013 but began to make minor electoral inroads in 2015 and 2016 by winning seats in state parliaments. But the most troubling impact of the accusatory rhetoric surrounding refugees was the accompanying violence meted out to them. By October 2015, there had been in that year almost 500 individual attacks on homes intended for refugees, the majority undertaken by locals with no previous criminal record.[19] In 2016, the interior ministry reported that there had been 3,533 attacks on migrants and hostels during the year – including 2,545 attacks on individual migrants. In one incident, a fire erupted at a building destined to house refugees.[20] Police reported that some onlookers sought to prevent firefighters from extinguishing the blaze, whilst others cheered.[21]

A Republican coup

The migrant crisis was a huge game-changer for the radical right in Europe, but perhaps a bigger change was occurring across the Atlantic. Donald Trump did not just stun the world in November 2016 upon his election as US President, his so-far brief political career has been met with dismay since its beginnings in 2015. Many were shocked by his high poll ratings before the Republican primary elections. People were baffled when he consistently brushed aside his opponents in the vote for delegates in the first half of 2016. There was disbelief when he won the primary and was declared presidential nominee in May 2016.

Trump dealt his greatest shock when he achieved victory in the presidential election on 8 November 2016. Whilst he lost the popular vote, Trump won in key swing states, gaining 304 electoral college votes to Democrat nominee Hillary Clinton's 227. Just over eight years since the country had elected its first African-American as President, Trump was inaugurated as the forty-fifth President of the United States on 20 January 2017.

The real estate tycoon's political interventions have been ever-present for decades. However, he rose to prominence as the figurehead of the so-called 'birther movement', which propagated the racist conspiracy theory that Barack Obama's birth certificate was fake and that he was not a US citizen. Since Obama's presidency began in 2009, anti-establishment sentiment – always a feature of US politics – had been visceral. Anti-government sentiment from the political right was most explicit within the Tea Party – a right-wing, conservative grass-roots movement hugely critical of Obama which became greatly influential in Republican politics.

Trump sought to tap into this anti-establishment sentiment when he announced his candidacy for the Republican primary elections in June 2015. He became quickly known for his braggadocio, swagger and nativist statements. He criticised Vietnam War torture victim and former presidential nominee John McCain, saying he 'likes people who weren't captured'. He claimed that Mexico was sending 'people that have lots of problems, and they're bringing those problems with us. They're bringing drugs. They're bringing crime. They're rapists. And some, I assume, are good people.'[22] He pledged to build a wall across the Mexican border, which he would force Mexico to pay for.

Trump advocated significant economic nationalism and was a proponent of anti-free trade policies such as withdrawal from the Trans-Pacific Partnership and the North American Free Trade Agreement. Through controversy, often created via his own Twitter account, he stole the limelight from other Republican nominees and easily won the Republican primary. When he accepted the presidential nomination at the Republican National Convention in May 2016, his acceptance speech displayed decidedly authoritarian tendencies; he bellowed 'We will also be a country of law and order!' He also demonstrated the anti-establishment statements common to the radical right, stating: 'Big business, elite media and major donors are lining up behind the campaign of my opponent because they know she will keep our rigged system in place.'[23]

Yet Trump was not, as yet, a populist. He tended to boast far more about himself than about 'the people'. He embarked on a populist strategy following the appointment in August 2006 of Stephen Bannon, CEO of far right Breitbart News and figurehead of the so-called 'alt-right' movement – a loose group of far right nationalists who had rejected mainstream conservatism. Matthew Feldman is sceptical of the label 'alt-right', arguing that it is effectively 'a synonym for white nationalism'. He likens it to a 'coat of white paint over asbestos' which is used 'because saying you are far right or fascist puts you in the political ghetto'. The use of the term, according to Feldman, is 'a way of distinguishing yourself from the traditional or mainstream right, but also obscures the fact that many of these people are revolutionaries'.[24]

Bannon, now the White House's chief strategist, is well read in the writings of the European far right, and is fond of the French Front National. He sought, in the words of conservative columnist Ben Shapiro, to 'transform conservatism into European far right nationalist populism'.[25] Trump's campaign remained nativist, xenophobic and authoritarian – a regular feature of the campaign was his promise to 'lock up' his opponent Hillary Clinton – but also took on a populist tone, making references to the people and contrasting them to a rotten establishment. He pledged to 'drain the swamp' of Washington DC, claiming it was full of corrupt elites, and hand power to ordinary people. Trump was propelled to the White House by older, white voters. Clinton won convincingly with voters under forty, whereas Trump was popular with over-fifties. White voters made up 70 per cent of the turnout and Trump won 58 per cent of them, gaining only 12 per cent of the black vote. Those educated at a lower level also tended to go for Trump: he won 51 per cent of those whose highest education level was high school. Trump's vote has been portrayed as a backlash from those left behind economically and from the working class who lost out from deindustrialisation, but in fact the poorest voters went for Hillary Clinton. She beat Trump by 12 per cent with voters on an income of less than $30,000 and by 9 per cent of those earning between $30,000 and $50,000. Trump won in all other income groups surveyed whose income was over $50,000.[26]

Much like the Brexit vote, Trump's vote reflected concerns over demographic change and anxieties about the changing character of national identity. The United States currently has a foreign-born population of 14 per cent. By 2055, it will no longer be a white-majority country and no single racial or ethnic group will be in the majority.[27] Amanda Taub, writing in the *New York Times*, described Trump's election as 'a crisis of white identity': 'Whiteness means being part of the group whose appearance, traditions, religion and even food are the default norm. It's being a person who, by unspoken rules, was long entitled as part of "us" instead of "them".'[28]

Whilst Trump won states in the former industrial heartland of the United States, now known as the 'rustbelt', economic factors appear to have less to do with his victory than the concern of white voters about losing their privilege in an ever-changing, ever-globalising world.

In spite of these early indicators, Donald Trump's election as US President will no doubt perplex scholars and historians for decades. However, what is certain is that he falls into the radical right category and is therefore of immense relevance. The extent of his populism can be found in his inaugural address of 20 January:

> Today's ceremony, however, has very special meaning because today we are not merely transferring power from one administration to another or from one party to another – but we are transferring power from Washington DC and giving it back to you, the people. For too long a small group in our nation's capital has reaped the rewards of government while the people have borne the cost. Washington flourished but the people did not share in its wealth. Politicians prospered but the jobs left and the factories closed. The establishment protected itself but not the citizens of our country. Their victories have not been your victories. Their triumphs have not been your triumphs. And while they celebrated in our nation's capital, there has been little to celebrate for struggling families all across our land. That all changes starting right here and right now because this moment is your moment. It belongs to you. It belongs to everyone gathered here today and everyone watching all across America.[29]

Matthew Feldman argues that whilst Trump's own ideology is little more than 'narcissism and self-aggrandisement', his pledge 'America First!' 'has very specific resonances to those familiar with US history' – referring to the pro-Nazi Charles Lindbergh and isolationist America First Committee which sought to keep the United States out of the Second World War. Trump is 'coming out of a very distinct American tradition', Feldman argues.[30]

Trump's electoral success however has not followed him into office. Since his Presidency began, his administration has been riddled by investigations into alleged collusion with the Russian state during the presidential election. Key policies such as the 'total ban' on Muslims entering the United States have been knocked back by the courts. Trump's ratings lie at historically low levels for a President elected a matter of months ago. In fact, since Trump's election several failures of the radical right in Europe have been witnessed. Geert Wilders' Party for Freedom was widely expected to win the most votes during the Dutch general election held in March, but instead came a distant second. Marine Le Pen topped the polls for months ahead of the French presidential election. Whilst she reached the second round of voting, she was resoundingly beaten by radical centrist Emmanuel Macron in May. Yet the sigh of relief expressed by many merely demonstrates how far the radical right have come – from the margins to the mainstream.

What this chapter has demonstrated is that the main-streaming of the far right is not limited to Britain. It is a phenomenon occurring throughout the western world. When we look into the past we can see how concern over migration and globalisation has assisted the rise of the far right in a range of countries. Far right support has now become normalised in Europe, and the United States has a radical right-wing President. Brexit has proven one of the biggest revolts we have seen so far, and has further demonstrated the growing insurgency and increased power of xenophobic politics across the continent.

CONCLUSION

The Brexit vote was decades in the making and its roots lie deep in British history. Since the nineteenth century, hostility to foreigners has been a regular feature of British life, as have political movements seeking to scapegoat and condemn them. Postwar immigration and the ethnic change it brought created a backlash from the public and gave it a new, racially charged political potency. The arrival of migrants from the Commonwealth changed the face of Britain, and has transformed it into the vibrant melting pot we witness today. Yet multicultural Britain has been met with anxiety by many, and with hostility by some.

Resentment over immigration has been present in sharp form since at least the 1960s but was kept under control by a political elite who recognised the explosive and divisive impact the politics of immigration could have on the fabric of society. Yet, as we arrived in the twenty-first century, despite Labour's promises of a multicultural Britain comfortable in its own skin, a concerted backlash was witnessed. Politicians were chastised for flooding the country with foreigners, while the treatment of immigrants in the press was, on a daily basis, full of hyperbole and anger. Politicians found themselves unable to change the narrative and often appeased the nationalist press and hard right politicians. Political movements until then, especially those on the far right, had generally failed to turn negative sentiment over immigration into votes or support. They were tainted by the fascist brand and all its baggage. The anti-fascist war generation saw little appeal in their extreme solutions.

Following the election of New Labour, the climate became more hospitable for the far right. Anti-immigration stories began to dominate the media and mainstream politicians often joined in. As the war generation declined, the BNP came along and embarked on a populist rebrand which appeared to break the fascist taboo that had existed in British politics since the 1920s. Immigration as an issue grew in importance for the public, yet the BNP would not be the benefactors. Public trust in politicians continued to corrode and upon the emergence of a more media-savvy, 'moderate' movement on the radical right, anti-immigration politics became increasingly normalised. The impact of Ukip has not been its electoral victories or public support per se, but its influence on the mainstream, which began to develop an anti-immigration, anti-elite consensus.

Britain is in danger of forgetting the lessons of history. When a paranoid, heightened national consciousness infects political debate at the expense of reason and tolerance, the consequences can be dire. The mainstreaming of the far right does not mean that those who hold fascist or Nazi ideologies are any more welcome in British politics. Brexit was neither preceded nor followed by a significant rise in support for totalitarian ideas or extreme political violence. Rather, the broader worldview of the far right, one which sees the 'nation' as the be-all and end-all in politics and seeks to scapegoat foreigners for Britain's problems, has become the new normal. The far right, as a movement, has failed but its ideas have become absorbed into the mainstream. The relentless criticism and stigmatisation of immigrants in British newspapers has become so common in Britain that many members of the public are simply desensitised to the message. A growing number of politicians and commentators seek not to allay the public's fears over immigration, globalisation and modernity, but exploit and inflame them.

Whilst the Brexit vote reflected the culmination of years of nationalist rhetoric in politics and the media, the process is still ongoing. One may believe that in an age of social media, the influence of the traditional press is dying. Newspaper circulation has dropped significantly in recent years. In 2001, around 3.6 million read *The Sun* per day; in 2017 this figure had more than halved to around 1.6 million. These figures can be slightly misleading, however, as many people simply consume their news online. MailOnline, the *Daily Mail*'s website, had over 4.1 billion views in 2015. Traditional forms of media such as TV, newspapers and the radio are still hugely important, and whilst politicians use social media frequently, newspapers in particular hold much sway over politicians.

The 2015 general election was predicted by many to be greatly influenced by social media, and to demonstrate the decline of the traditional media's influence on politics. Yet, as a report by Oxford University's Reuters Institute for the Study of Journalism said:

> Despite the millions of tweets, retweets, posts, likes, shares, and views, there is no evidence that social media played a decisive role either in boosting engagement and turnout, or in the election result. There is evidence that traditional media, and particularly broadcast media with their set piece debates and events, remained much more influential on voters.[1]

Those expecting the demise of the right-wing press as key drivers of anti-immigrant sentiment any time soon will be left disappointed.

That we have not seen the end of the mainstreaming of the far right should trouble us all. Immediately after the vote, Britain experienced a significant spike in hate crime. Just under 4,000 incidents were logged in July 2016 alone. Hate crime overall rose by almost 20 per cent in 2015–16 from the previous year. In August 2016, a Polish migrant, Arkadiusz Jóźwik, was murdered after a late-night attack in Harlow, Essex. It was an area where many migrants had experienced abuse following the Brexit vote and the incident was seen by some as indicative of a new toxic climate following the referendum.[2]

In Huntingdon, Cambridgeshire, laminated cards were left outside schools and homes saying 'no more Polish vermin'. A Polish community centre in Hammersmith, London was vandalised and graffitied with the words 'Go Home' shortly after the vote. These are but a few localised incidents, but many migrants have spoken of the fear they suffered after the vote, a feeling compounded by intimidation from extreme elements who voted to leave. Rhetoric has consequences and unknown outcomes, and the regular occurrence of divisive, xenophobic discourse in public life can have untold violent consequences for vulnerable minorities.

Perhaps even more troubling has been the response from the government and the *winning* side of the vote, which has sought to crush opposition and dissent in the name of 'democracy'. Following Theresa May's appointment as Prime Minister in July 2016, there was debate over whether Parliament should have a vote over triggering Article 50, which would mark the formal process of leaving the EU. City-based lawyer Gina Miller took the government to court on the grounds that it needed parliamentary consent to trigger Article 50, and the High Court of Justice ruled in her favour. Miller, who is British of Guyanese descent, was subjected to a torrent of racial abuse on social media, as well as death threats. *The Sun* described her as part of 'the loaded foreign elite' trying to stifle the will of the British people. Miller is a British citizen. The High Court judges who voted for Parliament to have a say were subjected to a tabloid witch-hunt. The *Daily Mail* emblazoned images of three of them on its front page coupled with the sinister headline 'Enemies of the People'.

The Conservative Party under Theresa May similarly embarked on a hard-line Brexit stance which sought to end British membership not just of the EU, but also the EU single market, purely to try and reduce immigration numbers. At the Conservative Party conference, May eschewed the opportunity to unite a deeply divided country in an attempt to rebrand herself as a populist railing against the 'elite'. She pledged to 'put the power of government squarely at the service of ordinary working-class people . . . because too often that isn't how it works today. Just listen to the way a lot of politicians and commentators talk about the public.'

Embarking on a slightly bizarre attack on a mythical pro-EU elite (of which surely she must be a part, as she was a Home Secretary campaigning to remain), and echoing William Hague's 2001 'foreign land' speech, she said: 'They find your patriotism distasteful, your concerns about immigration parochial, your views about crime illiberal, your attachment to your job security inconvenient. They find the fact that more than seventeen million voters decided to leave the European Union simply bewildering.' Failing to acknowledge that over 16 million voted to remain, May argued that 'too many people in positions of power behave as though they have more in common with international elites than with the people down the road, the people they employ, the people they pass in the street. But if you believe you're a citizen of the world, you're a citizen of nowhere.'[3]

There has however recently been a backlash towards the hard-line stance on Brexit of Theresa May's government. As the country formally enters negotiations to leave the European Union, it appears deeply divided in an increasingly unstable political climate. May's gamble, which saw her call a snap election held in June 2017, backfired spectacularly. The party, which sought a mandate for a 'hard Brexit', lost ground to Labour and crucially, its majority, winning 317 seats. Whilst a minority Conservative government limps on, the future is uncertain.

Jeremy Corbyn's Labour Party, committed to Brexit, but a softer version, were able to mobilise the young in their droves and may well have stalled British politics' lurch to the right which reached its apogee with the 2016 Brexit vote. Corbyn's success was indicative of the growing prominence of identity and values as opposed to economic interest – something we witnessed during the Brexit vote. The party gained thirty seats and a 10 per cent increase in vote share, driven by what polling expert Professor John Curtice referred to as a 'tsunami of support' from younger, professional, middle-class voters who plumped for Remain in the EU referendum.[4] The Conservative Party, who also increased their vote despite losing seats, gained a higher share of C2DE voters – the lowest socio-economic group – as well as those with less formal education, than Labour.[5]

The election also demonstrated further proof of the mainstreaming of the anti-immigrant, nationalist politics under investigation throughout this book. The Tories, committed to the 'hard Brexit' favoured largely only by the radical and extreme right until 2016, reaffirmed their pledge to reduce immigration to the 'tens of thousands', claiming in their manifesto that 'immigration is still too high' and 'it is difficult to build a cohesive society' with current immigration levels. The manifesto also focused heavily on security issues, claiming that 'in too many parts of our country, we have communities that are divided, often along racial or religious lines' and that 'our enjoyment of Britain's diversity must not prevent us from confronting the menace of extremism'. The alleged close relationship between multiculturalism and political extremism, ruthlessly pursued by the right-wing press since 9/11, appears to have now become received wisdom within the Conservative Party.

Through their co-option of radical right ideas, the party has not only stemmed the rise of Ukip but rendered them practically redundant. Ukip received just shy of 600,000 votes in the 2017 election (1.8 per cent) – a tiny proportion of their 2015 vote. The future indeed appears bleak for Ukip, who have had high-profile figures resign from the party in their droves. When their only MP, Douglas Carswell, quit the party in March 2017 and called for Brexiteers to vote Tory, asserting that Ukip's work was done, he was in a sense correct. Ukip may have failed but the ideas that propelled them to prominence most certainly have not and have found a new home in Theresa May's Conservative Party. The vote in June 2016 had little to do with the merits and demerits of EU membership. It reflected a public at the end of their tether with a political establishment perceived as out of touch with the concerns of ordinary Britons. Brexit has not acted as a 'safety valve' through which nativist sentiment against liberalism was drained. Rather, it has dragged the centre ground of British politics further to the right. The Conservative Party, on a radical right platform which promises to dramatically reduce immigration by taking Britain out of the European Union, is now at its most dominant in British politics since at least the 1980s, possibly even the 1930s. It cannot be seen as a surprise when one considers the historical context. Its familiarity, however, should not mitigate our concern. Brexit and the election of Donald Trump, as well as ascendant movements on the far right in Europe, pose the biggest threat to the liberal democratic order since the Second World War.

ACKNOWLEDGMENTS

Many people have helped with this project, but none more so than Nikki Griffiths at Melville House UK. Nikki has provided great assistance and been enthusiastic about the book from the very beginning, for which I am very grateful. I would also like to thank Dennis Johnson at Melville House in New York for his support for the book.

I would like to express my gratitude to my academic mentor and friend, Professor Matthew Feldman, whose continued support during the writing of the book has been a big help. I must also thank other academics who have greatly improved the book with their wisdom: Dr Joe Mulhall, Professor David Feldman, Professor Eric Kaufmann, Dr Aurélien Mondon, Professor Colin Holmes, Professor Stefaan Walgrave and Professor Sarah de Lange. I would like to thank all those I met and interviewed during my travels through England researching for the book, particularly Members of Parliament who spared their valuable time to chat with me: Dan Jarvis, Melanie Onn, Peter Aldous, Douglas Carswell and Matt Warman. I would also like to thank the local councillors I spoke to, including Christopher Akers-Belcher, Allen Cowles, Paul Hague, Peter Bedford, Michael Brookes, Graham Plant and Bert Poole.

Finally, thanks go out to my family: Keith, Corinne and Jill, who have always been supportive and encouraging of me. My biggest thanks are for Riina, who has been at the coalface putting up with me during the writing of this book, providing intellectual assistance as well as her love and support.

NOTES

1 Introduction

1 https://www.jrf.org.uk/report/
  brexit-vote-explained-poverty-low-skills-and-lack-opportunities
2 http://ukpollingreport.co.uk/blog/archives/9767
3 http://lordashcroftpolls.com/2016/06/
  how-the-united-kingdom-voted-and-why/
4 https://www.jrf.org.uk/report/
  brexit-vote-explained-poverty-low-skills-and-lack-opportunities
5 http://www.thetimes.co.uk/article/
  the-great-british-dividesomewheres-v-anywheres-s8qm908fo
6 http://lordashcroftpolls.com/2016/06/
  how-the-united-kingdom-voted-and-why/
7 http://lordashcroftpolls.com/2016/06/
  how-the-united-kingdom-voted-and-why/
8 http://blogs.lse.ac.uk/politicsandpolicy/
  personal-values-brexit-vote/
9 http://www.ethnicity.ac.uk/medialibrary/briefings/
  dynamicsofdiversity/how-has-ethnic-diversity-
  grown-1991-2001-2011.pdf
10 http://blogs.lse.ac.uk/europpblog/2017/05/30/
  uk-voters-including-leavers-care-more-about-reducing-non-eu-
  than-eu-migration/
11 Cas Mudde, 'Definitions', *Hope not Hate*, January–February 2016,
  p. 6.

1 A History of Intolerance

1 http://www.margaretthatcher.org/speeches/displaydocument.
asp?docid=107246

2 https://www.gov.uk/government/news/
british-values-article-by-david-cameron

3 Interview with Professor Colin Holmes.

4 Roy Foster, *Modern Ireland: 1600–1972* (London, 1989), p. 345.

5 *The Times*, 2 April 1847.

6 Quoted in Lewis Curtis, *Anglo-Saxons and Celts: A Study of Anti-Irish Prejudice in Victorian England* (New York, 1968), p. 51.

7 Mo Moulton, *Ireland and the Irish in Interwar England* (Cambridge, 2014), p. 295.

8 https://www.theguardian.com/uk-news/2015/mar/04/
ukip-nigel-farage-immigrants-british-brothers-league

9 http://www.uniset.ca/naty/aliensact1905.pdf

10 Interview with Professor David Feldman.

11 Winston Churchill, 'Zionism versus Bolshevism', *Illustrated Sunday Herald*, 8 February 1920.

12 Interview with Professor Matthew Feldman.

13 Nesta Webster, *World Revolution: The Plot Against Civilisation* (London, 1921), p. 161.

14 David Edgar, 'Racism, Fascism and the Politics of the National Front', *Race and Class* 19 (1977), p. 116.

15 *The Blackshirt*, 24 January 1936; *Action*, 21 May 1936.

16 *The Blackshirt*, 18 January 1935.

17 Interview with Professor Matthew Feldman.

18 Metropolitan Police Special Branch Report, 8 August 1947, p. 2. National Archives, Kew, London: HO 45/24469/Part 2.

19 *Union*, 22 May 1948.

20 The Mau Mau were a loose organisation who undertook violent

resistance to British colonial rule, their recruits coming largely from Kenya's dominant Kikuyu tribe.

21 Peter Fryer, *Staying Power: The History of Black People in Britain* (London, 1984), p. 374.

22 Winston Churchill, quoted in Randall Hansen, *Citizenship and Immigration in Postwar Britain* (Oxford, 2004), p. 3.

23 Interview with Dr Joe Mulhall.

24 Transcript of interview with John Tyndall conducted by David Baker, 4 April 1978. A.K. Chesterton Collection, Bath University Archive: A.11.

25 Roger Eatwell, *Fascism* (London, 2003), p. 334.

26 Interview with Dr Joe Mulhall.

2   Britain's Multiracial Society and the Failure of Extremism

1 Gallup Poll, 1958 in G. Gallup (ed.), *The Gallup International Public Opinion Polls: Great Britain 1937–1975*, Volume 1 (New York, 1976), pp. 477–8.

2 *The Guardian*, 3 September 1958.

3 Interview with Professor David Feldman.

4 Interview with Professor Colin Holmes.

5 Grantley Adams quoted in James Hampshire, *Citizenship and Belonging: Immigration and the Politics of Demographic Governance in Postwar Britain* (Basingstoke, 2005), p. 70.

6 Gallup Poll, 1963 in Gallup, *The Gallup International Public Opinion Polls*, Vol. 1, p. 703.

7 Gallup Poll, 1965 in Gallup, *The Gallup International Public Opinion Polls*, Vol. 2, p. 803; Gallup Poll, 1969 in Gallup, *The Gallup International Public Opinion Polls*, Vol. 2, p. 1032.

8 Gallup Poll, 1965 in Gallup, *The Gallup International Public*

Opinion Polls, Vol. 2, p. 823; Gallup Poll, 1968 in Gallup, *The Gallup International Public Opinion Polls*, Vol. 2, p. 984.

9   Martin Walker, *The National Front* (Glasgow, 1977), pp. 53–5.

10 Quoted in Erik Bleich, *Race Politics in Britain and France: Ideas and Policymaking since the 1960s* (Cambridge, 2003), p. 48.

11 Enoch Powell, cited in Walker, *The National Front*, p. 108.

12 Gallup Poll, 1965 in Gallup, *The Gallup International Public Opinion Polls*, Vol. 2, p. 803.

13 Gallup Poll, 1967 in Gallup, *The Gallup International Public Opinion Polls*, Vol. 2, pp. 949–50.

14 http://www.telegraph.co.uk/comment/3643823/Enoch-Powells-Rivers-of-Blood-speech.html

15 Interview with Professor David Feldman.

16 Interview with Professor David Feldman.

17 NOP Poll, 1968, cited in M. Collins, 'Immigration and opinion polls in postwar Britain', *Modern History Review*, 18(4), pp. 8–13.

18 Gallup Poll, 1968 in Gallup, *The Gallup International Public Opinion Polls*, Vol. 2, p. 984.

19 http://www.express.co.uk/news/uk/418261/Ukip-leader-Nigel-Farage-says-Enoch-Powell-s-River-of-Blood-speech-was-a-disaster

20 Walker, *The National Front*, p. 111.

21 Gallup Poll, 1972 in Gallup, *The Gallup International Public Opinion Polls*, Vol. 2, p. 1199.

22 NOP Poll, 1978 cited in M. Collins, 'Immigration and opinion polls in postwar Britain', *Modern History Review*, 18(4), pp. 8–13.

23 *The Times*, 4 February 1960.

24 *The Times*, 31 August 1972.

25 Walker, *The National Front*, p. 134.

26 *The Times*, 15 June 1975.

27 http://archive.spectator.co.uk/article/23rd-april-1977/12/
national-front-moves-on-london

28 *The Times*, 2 July 1976.

29 *The Times*, 30 August 1977.

30 http://www.margaretthatcher.org/document/103485

31 NOP Poll, 1978 cited in Collins, 'Immigration and opinion polls
in postwar Britain.'

32 http://www.margaretthatcher.org/document/103485

33 Interview with Professor Colin Holmes.

3 Far Right Mainstreaming, Mainstreaming the Far Right

1 Nigel Copsey, *Contemporary British Fascism: The British National
Party and the Quest for Legitimacy* (Basingstoke, 2008), pp. 76–99.

2 http://news.bbc.co.uk/hi/english/static/audio_video/
programmes/panorama/transcripts/transcript_30_06_00.txt

3 Interview with Professor Matthew Feldman.

4 https://www.theguardian.com/uk/2005/jul/20/otherparties.
thefarright

5 John Tyndall, quoted in Walker, *The National Front*, p. 116.

6 *Identity*, October–November 2000.

7 *Identity*, October–November 2000.

8 *Patriot*, Spring 1999.

9 Griffin quoted in Copsey, *Contemporary British Fascism*, p. 157.

10 https://www.theguardian.com/media/2002/feb/25/
pressandpublishing.falklands

11 Labour Party manifesto, 1997.

12 UNHCR Global Trends Report, 2015, p. 6.

13 http://www.migrationobservatory.ox.ac.uk/resources/briefings/
migration-to-the-uk-asylum/

14 http://www.independent.co.uk/news/warning-to-editors-on-racist-reports-1191857.html

15 'Victims of Intolerance', *Refugees*, vol. 1 no. 142 (2006).

16 Scott Blinder, 'Imagined Immigration: The Impact of Different Meanings of "Immigrants" in Public Opinion and Policy Debates in Britain', *Political Studies*, vol. 63 (2013), p. 88.

17 https://www.theguardian.com/media/2003/feb/03/mondaymediasection.politicsandthemedia

18 Charlie Brooker's *Newswipe*, BBC4, 1 May 2009.

19 *Daily Mail*, 9 December 2002.

20 *Daily Express*, 19 May 2006.

21 *Daily Express*, 29 November 2002.

22 *Daily Express*, 25 January 2005.

23 *Daily Mail*, 29 November 2002.

24 https://www.ipsos-mori.com/researchpublications/researcharchive/1061/Attitudes-towards-Asylum-Seekers-for-Refugee-Week.aspx#note1

25 https://www.ipsos-mori.com/researchpublications/researcharchive/1639/Britain-Today-Are-We-An-Intolerant-Nation.aspx

26 *Daily Star*, 8 March 2005.

27 *Daily Telegraph*, 15 June 2003.

28 *Daily Express*, 6 August 2004.

29 *Daily Star*, 8 March 2005.

30 'Asylum Seekers – Meeting Their Healthcare Needs', British Medical Association Report (London, 2002).

31 *Daily Express*, 27 July 2005.

32 *Sunday People*, 4 March 2001.

33 *Daily Express*, 29 July 2004.

34 *Daily Star*, 2 March 2005.

35 https://www.theguardian.com/uk/2001/mar/01/immigration.
    immigrationandpublicservices

36 *Daily Express*, 15 November 2002.

37 *Daily Express*, 16 November 2005.

38 *Daily Mail*, 6 December 2002.

39 *Daily Mail*, 11 December 2002.

40 https://www.ipsos-mori.com/researchpublications/
    researcharchive/1639/Britain-Today-Are-We-An-Intolerant-
    Nation.aspx

41 *The Sun*, 7 March 2001.

42 *Daily Star*, 18 December 2002.

43 *Daily Mail*, 1 February 2001.

44 *Daily Mail*, 31 December 2002.

45 *Daily Mail*, 10 September 2003.

46 'Understanding the decision-making of asylum seekers', Home
    Office Research Study 243, p. viii.

47 *Identity*, January–February 2000.

4   The Rise and Fall of the BNP

1   Tony Blair speech on Millennium Dome, 24 February 1998.

2   Labour Party manifesto, 1997.

3   https://www.theguardian.com/world/2001/apr/19/race.
    britishidentity

4   https://www.theguardian.com/politics/2001/mar/04/
    conservatives.speeches

5   http://www.telegraph.co.uk/news/uknews/1325520/Kennedy-
    attacks-Powellesque-Hague-over-asylum.html

6   http://www.dailymail.co.uk/columnists/article-117581/Peter-
    Hitchens-The-Tories-try-Guardianistas-the---BNP-prosper.
    html

7   http://www.dailymail.co.uk/columnists/article-117581/Peter-
    Hitchens-The-Tories-try-Guardianistas-the---BNP-prosper.html

8   *Identity*, March–April 2000.

9   *Daily Express*, 29 April 2003.

10 http://www.dailymail.co.uk/columnists/article-228320/
    This-sinister-sect-creeps-misfits-racists-soon-bigger-threat-
    Labour-Tories-.html

11 *The Sun*, 15 July 2004.

12 http://www.telegraph.co.uk/news/uknews/
    immigration/10445585/Labour-made-a-spectacular-mistake-
    on-immigration-admits-Jack-Straw.html

13 Carlos Vargas-Silva, 'Long-term international migration flows to
    and from the United Kingdom', Migration Observatory Report,
    2016.

14 https://www.theguardian.com/media/2008/mar/15/dailymail.
    pressandpublishing

15 Robert Ford, Gareth Morrell & Anthony Heath, '"Fewer but
    better?": Public views towards immigration', British Social
    Attitudes Survey no. 29, 2012, p. 26.

16 Paul Golding quoted in Nigel Copsey and Graham Macklin, *The
    British National Party: Contemporary Perspectives* (Abingdon,
    2011), p. 82.

17 *Spearhead*, April 2004.

18 https://www.theguardian.com/politics/2003/apr/30/thefarright.
    elections2003

19 http://news.bbc.co.uk/1/hi/uk_politics/vote_2005/
    frontpage/4430453.stm

20 *The Spectator*, 1 December 2007.

21 Interview with Dr Aurélien Mondon.

22 M. Phillips, *Londonistan: How Britain is Creating a Terror State
    from Within* (London, 2006), p. 110.

23 Phillips, *Londonistan*, p. 111.

24 Phillips, *Londonistan*, p. 107.

25 Phillips, *Londonistan*, p. 122.

26 http://www.spectator.co.uk/2007/07/the-public-know-how-these-attacks-happen-unlike-the-politicians/

27 http://www.telegraph.co.uk/news/uknews/1539367/We-need-a-United-Kingdom.html

28 *The Spectator*, 16 December 2006.

29 http://www.dailymail.co.uk/columnists/article-385587/BNP-voters-arent-Barking--theyre-just-mad-Labour.html

30 http://www.melaniephillips.com/the-troika-of-bigotry

31 http://www.melaniephillips.com/an-offensive-reaction

32 http://www.dailymail.co.uk/debate/article-1177535/HARRY-PHIBBS-Its-Tories-disastrous-government-blame-rise-BNP.html

33 http://www.telegraph.co.uk/comment/personal-view/5363715/We-have-nothing-to-fear-from-these-British-National-Party-jokers.html

34 https://www.ipsos-mori.com/researchpublications/researcharchive/2349/Ipsos-MORI-Expenses-Poll-for-the-BBC.aspx

35 http://www.dailymail.co.uk/debate/article-1181668/MARTIN-SAMUEL-Protest-vote-Vote-fascist-fascist-.html

36 http://www.dailymail.co.uk/debate/article-1186775/DAILY-MAIL-COMMENT-The-truly-nasty-party.html

37 *Identity*, January–February 2000.

38 http://www.dailymail.co.uk/debate/article-1191750/ANALYSIS-Nick-Griffin--bully-got-away-it.html

39 http://www.dailymail.co.uk/debate/article-1191736/Labour-vacuum-let-bigots.html

40 http://www.dailymail.co.uk/debate/article-1222355/Nick-Griffin-Repugnant-slippery-exposed-vessel.html

41 http://www.dailymail.co.uk/debate/article-1222622/Nick-Griffin-The-ogre-panto.html

42 http://www.dailymail.co.uk/debate/article-1222623/BBC-trial-taught-nothing.html

43 http://www.telegraph.co.uk/news/politics/6417906/One-in-four-would-consider-voting-BNP.html

44 Andrew Rawnsley, *The End of the Party: The Rise and Fall of New Labour* (London, 2010), p. 730.

45 Nigel Copsey, *The English Defence League: Challenging our country and our values of social inclusion, fairness and equality*. Faith Matters Report (London, 2010), p. 5.

46 Robinson's actual name is Stephen Yaxley-Lennon.

47 https://www.theguardian.com/uk-news/the-northerner/2014/may/12/english-defence-league-march-in-rotherham-cost-1m

48 https://rusi.org/commentary/was-anders-breivik-psychotic-spree-killer-or-calculating-terrorist

49 http://www.newstatesman.com/2009/07/mehdi-hasan-muslim-terrorism-white-british

50 http://www.newstatesman.com/2009/07/mehdi-hasan-muslim-terrorism-white-british

51 http://www.telegraph.co.uk/comment/6425004/The-BNP-can-be-dismissed-but-their-constituency-can-not.html

5 Breaking Point: Enter Ukip

1 Nigel Farage, *Flying Free* (London, 2011), p. 133.

2 Farage, *Flying Free*, p. 108.

3 Ukip 2009 European Parliament Elections manifesto.

4 http://www.telegraph.co.uk/news/uknews/1463248/Howard-rages-at-UKIP-gadflies.html

5 http://news.bbc.co.uk/1/hi/4875026.stm

6 http://www.telegraph.co.uk/news/politics/ukip/10735155/Nigel-Farage-I-am-proud-to-have-taken-a-third-of-the-BNPs-support.html

7 Matthew Goodwin and Robert Ford, *Revolt on the Right: Explaining Support for the Radical Right in Britain* (Abingdon, 2014), p. 11.

8 http://www.thetimes.co.uk/article/books-revolting-how-the-establishment-are-undermining-democracy-and-what-theyre-afraid-of-by-mick-hume-5m76qkh92

9 Cas Mudde, 'The populist radical right: a pathological normalcy', *West European Politics* 33:6 (2010), p. 1173.

10 Ruth Wodak, 'Anything Goes! – The Haiderization of Europe' in *Right-Wing Populism in Europe: Politics and Discourse*, ed. Ruth Wodak, Majid Khosravinik and Brigitte Mral (London, 2013), pp. 27–8.

11 Interview with Professor Sarah de Lange.

12 Interview with Professor Stefaan Walgrave.

13 Conservative Party manifesto, 2010.

14 https://yougov.co.uk/news/2014/10/29/political-disaffection-not-new-it-rising-and-drivi/

15 https://www.ipsos-mori.com/researchpublications/researcharchive/3369/People-in-western-countries-pessimistic-about-future-for-young-people.aspx

16 Interview with Professor David Feldman.

17 http://www.newstatesman.com/blogs/the-staggers/2011/02/terrorism-islam-ideology

18 http://www.economist.com/blogs/bagehot/2011/02/britain_and_multiculturalism

19 http://www.economist.com/news/britain/21692886-eu-
    renegotiation-has-made-unlikely-diplomat-david-cameron-
    britains-new-ambassadors

20 https://www.gov.uk/government/uploads/system/uploads/
    attachment_data/file/251909/Quantitative_Assessment_
    of_Visitor_and_Migrant_Use_of_the_NHS_in_England_-_
    Exploring_the_Data_-_FULL_REPORT.pdf

21 https://www.demos.co.uk/files/
    JamesBrokenshireSpeechtoDemos.pdf

22 *The Times*, 8 March 2014.

23 https://yougov.co.uk/news/2012/12/17/
    perilous-politics-immigration/

24 https://yougov.co.uk/news/2013/05/08/
    immigration-concern-hits-three-year-high/

25 http://lordashcroftpolls.com/wp-content/uploads/2013/08/
    LORD-ASHCROFT-Public-opinion-and-the-politics-of-
    immigration2.pdf

26 http://www.express.co.uk/news/uk/129288/Keep-out-Britain-
    is-full-up; http://www.dailystar.co.uk/news/latest-news/331393/
    Britain-full-to-bursting-with-immigrants

27 http://www.niesr.ac.uk/blog/immigration-and-wages-getting-
    numbers-right#.WL7Et_KlTIU

28 http://cep.lse.ac.uk/pubs/download/brexit05.pdf

29 Interview with Professor David Feldman.

30 *Daily Express*, 26 August 2006.

31 *Sunday Express*, 10 August 2006.

32 http://www.migrationobservatory.ox.ac.uk/resources/reports/
    the-minimum-income-requirement-for-non-eea-family-
    members-in-the-uk/

33 *The Guardian*, 12 February 2013.

34 http://www.thetimes.co.uk/tto/news/politics/article3638941.ece

35 http://www.dailymail.co.uk/news/article-2280294/
The-mafia-bosses-wait-flood-Britain-beggars-While-
politicians-dither-new-wave-immigration-Eastern-
Europe-ruthless-gangmasters-rubbing-hands-
glee.html

36 http://www.dailymail.co.uk/news/article-2279419/
We-want-country-locks-door-Shocking-investigation-coming-
wave-immigration-Romania-Bulgaria.html

37 http://www.express.co.uk/comment/columnists/
patrick-o-flynn/378116/An-immigration-calamity-looms

38 *Daily Star*, 24 December 2013.

39 *Daily Express*, 29 December 2013.

40 *Daily Star*, 1 January 2014.

41 Farage interview with James O'Brien, LBC, May 2014.

42 http://www.dailymail.co.uk/debate/article-2992574/
Racist-No-Nigel-Farage-simply-stating-obvious-writes-
RICHARD-LITTLEJOHN.html

43 http://www.dailymail.co.uk/debate/article-2316746/RICHARD-
LITTLEJOHN-How-protest-ballot-box.html

44 http://www.dailymail.co.uk/debate/article-2319152/SIMON-
HEFFER-Theres-way-Dave-stub-Farage.html

45 https://www.thesun.co.uk/archives/news/9453/a-charlie-
hebdo-attack-here-would-help-put-nigel-farage-in-no10/

46 https://www.thetimes.co.uk/article/
ukip-isnt-a-protest-its-a-counter-revolution-xjrbb9wmj7n

47 http://www.independent.co.uk/voices/comment/editors-letter-
in-which-i-defend-giving-mr-farage-a-weekly-column-9027550.
html

6   Take Back Control: The EU Referendum

1   *The Sun*, 17 April 2015.
2   https://www.theguardian.com/world/2015/jan/08/
    paris-attack-nigel-farage-gross-policy-multiculturalism
3   https://www.theguardian.com/politics/2015/nov/16/
    nigel-farage-accuse-british-muslims-conflicting-loyalties
4   https://www.theguardian.com/politics/2016/feb/21/iain-duncan-
    smith-uk-risks-paris-style-attacks-by-staying-in-the-eu
5   http://www.telegraph.co.uk/news/politics/nigel-farage/11836131/
    Nigel-Farage-EU-has-opened-doors-to-migration-exodus-of-
    biblical-proportions.html
6   *The Times*, 10 September 2015.
7   http://www.dailymail.co.uk/news/article-3321431/MAC-Europe-
    s-open-borders.html
8   Interview with Dan Jarvis MP.
9   http://www.voteleavetakecontrol.org/pm_challenged_to_set_
    out_the_facts_on_eu_immigration.html
10 http://www.dailymail.co.uk/wires/pa/article-3603214/Turkey-
    course-join-EU-year-3000-insists-David-Cameron.html
11 https://www.theguardian.com/politics/2016/may/21/
    vote-leave-prejudice-turkey-eu-security-threat
12 Interview with Dr Joe Mulhall.
13 https://www.theguardian.com/commentisfree/2016/jun/18/
    eu-referendum-vote-leave-campaign-poisonous
14 http://blogs.spectator.co.uk/2016/06/a-day-of-infamy/

7   The Decline of England

1   http://www.migrationobservatory.ox.ac.uk/resources/briefings/
    uk-public-opinion-toward-migration-determinants-of-attitudes/

2   http://www.migrationobservatory.ox.ac.uk/resources/briefings/
    uk-public-opinion-toward-migration-determinants-of-
    attitudes/

3   https://www.gov.uk/government/uploads/system/uploads/
    attachment_data/file/465791/English_Indices_of_
    Deprivation_2015_-_Statistical_Release.pdf

4   Interview with Cllr Christopher Akers-Belcher.

5   Interview with Dan Jarvis MP.

6   Interview with Melanie Onn MP.

7   Interview with Cllr Christopher Akers-Belcher.

8   Interview with Wakefield politician.

9   Interview with Dan Jarvis.

10 Interview with Melanie Onn.

11 http://www.rotherhamadvertiser.co.uk/news/view,rotherham-
    among-britains-most-vulnerable-towns-report_18466.htm

12 Interview with Cllr Allen Cowles.

13 Interview with Cllr Paul Hague.

14 Social Impact of Population Change.

15 http://www.dailymail.co.uk/news/article-2037877/Boston-
    Lincolngrad-The-strange-transformation-sleepy-English-town.
    htm

16 Interview with Cllr Peter Bedford.

17 Interview with Cllr Michael Brookes.

18 Interview with Matt Warman MP.

19 https://www.great-yarmouth.gov.uk/CHttpHandler.
    ashx?id=988&p=0

20 Interview with Cllr Graham Plant.

21 Interview with Peter Aldous MP.

22 Interview with Cllr Bert Poole.

23 The 69.5 per cent figure is for the whole of the Tendring District
    Area.

24 Carswell left the party in March 2016 and did not stand in the 2017 general election.

25 *The Times*, 6 September 2014.

26 Interview with Douglas Carswell MP.

27 http://www.dailymail.co.uk/news/election/article-1267767/ General-Election-2010-David-Cameron-strip-MPs-perks-clean-politics.html

8 A Western Disease

1 Interview with Professor Eric Kaufmann.

2 Hans-Georg Betz, *Radical Right-Wing Populism in Western Europe* (New York, 1994), p. 93.

3 Interview with Dr Aurélien Mondon.

4 http://www.liberation.fr/evenement/2002/04/23/ votez-escroc-pas-facho_401301

5 http://www.volkskrant.nl/binnenland/pim-fortuyn-op-herhaling-de-islam-is-een-achterlijke-cultuur~a611698/

6 http://www.bbc.co.uk/news/world-europe-11469579

7 Interview with Dr Joe Mulhall.

8 http://www.hungarianhistory.com/lib/ebnerslota.pdf

9 http://trends.gmfus.org/files/2011/12/TTImmigration_final_web1.pdf

10 http://trends.gmfus.org/files/2014/09/Trends_Immigration_2014_web.pdf

11 http://www.pewglobal.org/2014/05/12/ chapter-3-most-support-limiting-immigration/

12 http://www.pewglobal.org/2016/07/11/ negative-views-of-minorities-refugees-common-in-eu/

13 https://www.washingtonpost.com/ news/worldviews/wp/2015/01/08/

europes-far-right-on-the-paris-attack-we-told-you-so/?utm_
term=.debocc810687

14 https://euobserver.com/justice/128941

15 Interview with Professor Sarah de Lange.

16 https://www.theguardian.com/world/2015/sep/03/
migration-crisis-hungary-pm-victor-orban-europe-response-
madness

17 http://europe.newsweek.com/national-fronts-marine-
le-pen-says-majority-refugees-are-economic-migrants-
332659

18 http://www.pewresearch.org/fact-tank/2016/09/16/
european-opinions-of-the-refugee-crisis-in-5-charts/

19 http://www.bbc.co.uk/news/world-europe-34487562

20 http://www.bbc.co.uk/news/world-europe-39096833

21 http://www.bbc.co.uk/news/world-europe-35625595

22 http://www.nydailynews.com/news/politics/
trump-outrageous-comments-mexicans-article-1.2773214

23 http://www.politico.com/story/2016/07/full-transcript-donald-
trump-nomination-acceptance-speech-at-rnc-225974

24 Interview with Professor Matthew Feldman.

25 http://www.dailywire.com/news/10770/3-thoughts-
steve-bannon-white-house-chief-ben-shapiro?utm_
source=twitter&utm_medium=social&utm_
content=news&utm_campaign=twitterbenshapiro

26 http://uk.businessinsider.com/exit-polls-who-voted-for-trump-
clinton-2016-11?r=US&IR=T/#more-women-voted-for-clinton-
as-expected-but-trump-still-got-42-of-female-votes-1

27 http://www.pewresearch.org/fact-tank/2016/03/31/10-
demographic-trends-that-are-shaping-the-u-s-and-the-world/

28 https://www.nytimes.com/2016/11/02/world/americas/brexit-
donald-trump-whites.html?_r=0

29 http://www.independent.co.uk/news/world/americas/donald-
    trump-inauguration-speech-transcript-text-full-read-a7538131.
    html
30 Interview with Professor Matthew Feldman.

Conclusion

1 http://reutersinstitute.politics.ox.ac.uk/sites/default/files/
   The%20Relationship%20between%20Traditional%2C%20
   New%20Media%20and%20the%20Electorate.pdf
2 https://www.theguardian.com/commentisfree/2016/sep/05/
   death-arkadiusz-jozwik-post-referendum-racism-xenophobes-
   brexit-vote
3 http://www.telegraph.co.uk/news/2016/10/05/
   theresa-mays-conference-speech-in-full/
4 http://www.cityam.com/267017/
   labours-election-result-driven-tsunami-professional-middle
5 https://yougov.co.uk/news/2017/06/13/
   how-britain-voted-2017-general-election/

FURTHER READING

Baker, David. *Ideology of Obsession: A.K. Chesterton and British Fascism* (1996)

Bale, Tim. *Five Year Mission: The Labour Party under Ed Miliband* (2015)

Bale, Tim. *The Conservative Party: From Thatcher to Cameron* (2010)

Bangstad, Sindre. *Anders Breivik and the Rise of Islamophobia* (2014)

Banks, Arron. *The Bad Boys of Brexit* (2016)

Bennett, Owen. *The Brexit Club: The Inside Story of the Leave Campaign's Shock Victory* (2016)

Betz, Hans-Georg. *Radical Right-Wing Populism in Western Europe* (1994)

Bleich, Erik. *Race Politics in Britain and France: Ideas and Policymaking since the 1960s* (2003)

Briggs, A. and Clavin, P. *Modern Europe: 1789–Present* (2003)

Campbell, Alastair. *The Alastair Campbell Diaries Vol. II: Power and the People, 1997–1999* (2011)

Campbell, Alastair. *The Alastair Campbell Diaries Vol. III: Power and Responsibility, 1999-2001* (2011)

Clegg, Nick. *Politics: Between the Extremes* (2016)

Copsey, N. & Macklin, G. (eds). *British National Party: Contemporary Perspectives* (2011)

Copsey, Nigel. *Anti-Fascism in Britain* (2016).

Copsey, Nigel. *Contemporary British Fascism: The British National Party and the Quest for Legitimacy* (2008)

D'Ancona, Matthew. *In It Together: The Inside Story of the Coalition Government* (2014)

Dunt, Ian. *Brexit: What the Hell Happens Now?* (2016)

Eatwell, Roger. *Fascism* (2003)

Evans, Eric. *Thatcher and Thatcherism* (2004)

Farage, Nigel. *Flying Free* (2011)

Farage, Nigel. *The Purple Revolution: The Year that Changed Everything* (2015)

Foster, Roy. *Modern Ireland: 1600–1972* (1989)

Fryer, Peter. *Staying Power: The History of Black People in Britain* (1984)

Gallup, George.(ed.) *The Gallup International Public Opinion Polls: Great Britain 1937–1975*, Volumes I & II (New York, 1976)

Gibbon, Gary. *Breaking Point: The UK Referendum on the EU and its Aftermath* (2016)

Goodhart, David. *The British Dream: Successes and Failures of Postwar Immigration* (2014)

Goodhart, David. *The Road to Somewhere: The Populist Revolt and the Future of Politics* (2017)

Goodwin, M. & Clarke, H. *Brexit: Why Britain Voted to Leave the European Union* (2017)

Goodwin, M. & Ford, R. *Revolt on the Right: Explaining Support for the Radical Right in Britain* (2014)

Hampshire, James. *Citizenship and Belonging: Immigration and the Politics of Demographic Governance in Postwar Britain* (2005)

Hansen, Randall. *Citizenship and Immigration in Postwar Britain* (2004)

Hennessy, Peter. *Having it So Good: Britain in the Fifties* (2006)

Holmes, Colin. *A Tolerant Country?: Immigrants, Refugees and Minorities* (1991)

Holmes, Colin. *John Bull's Island: Immigration and British Society, 1871–1971* (1988)

Jones, Owen. *Chavs: The Demonization of the Working Class* (2012)

Judt, Tony. *Postwar: A History of Europe Since 1945* (2010)

Kirby, M.W. *The Decline of British Economic Power Since 1870* (1981)

Macshane, Denis. *Brexit: How Britain Left Europe* (2016)

Mosbacher, M. & Wiseman, O. *Brexit Revolt: How the UK Voted to Leave the EU* (2016)

Moulton, Mo. *Ireland and the Irish in Interwar England* (2014)

Mudde, Cas. *On Extremism and Democracy in Europe* (2017)

Mudde, Cas. *Populism: A Very Short Introduction* (2017)

Mudde, Cas. *Populist Radical Right Parties in Europe* (2007)

Mudde, Cas. *The Populist Radical Right: A Reader* (2016)

Mullin, Chris. *A View From the Foothills* (2010)

Mullin, Chris. *A Walk-On Part: Diaries, 1994–1999* (2012)

Oliver, Craig. *Unleashing Demons: The Inside Story of Brexit* (2016)

Panayi, Panikos. *An Immigration History of Britain: Multicultural Racism since 1800* (2009)

Payne, Stanley. *A History of Fascism, 1914-1945* (1996)

Phillips, Melanie. *Londonistan: How Britain is Creating a Terror State from Within* (2006)

Phillips, M. & Phillips, T. *Windrush: The Irresistible Rise of Multi-Racial Britain* (2009)

Pugh, Martin. *'Hurrah for the Blackshirts!' Fascists and Fascism in Britain Between the Wars* (2006)

Pugh, Martin. *Speak for Britain! A New History of the Labour Party* (2011)

Rawnsley, Andrew. *Servants of the People: The Inside Story of New Labour* (2001)

Rawnsley, Andrew. *The End of the Party: The Rise and Fall of New Labour* (2010)

Schofield, Camilla. *Enoch Powell and the Making of Postcolonial Britain* (2015)

Schwarz, Bill. *The White Man's World* (2013)

Seldon, A. & Lodge G. *Brown at 10* (2011)

Seldon, Anthony. *Blair's Britain* (2007)

Seldon, Anthony. *Cameron at 10: The Verdict* (2016)

Seldon, Anthony. *The Coalition Effect* (2015)

Seymour, Richard. *Corbyn: The Strange Rebirth of Radical Politics* (2016)

Shipman, Tim. *All Out War: The Full Story of How Brexit Sank Britain's Political Class* (2016)

Simms, Brendan. *Britain's Europe: A Thousand Years of Conflict and Cooperation* (2017)

Sked, A. & Cook, C. *Post-War Britain, 1945–1992* (1993)

Stewart, Graham. *Bang! A History of Britain in the 1980s* (2014)

Stone, Dan. *Goodbye to All That? The Story of Europe since 1945* (2014)

Straw, Jack. *Last Man Standing: Memoirs of a Political Survivor* (2013)

Thurlow, Richard. *Fascism in Britain: From Oswald Mosley's Blackshirts to the National Front* (1987)

Toye, Richard. *Churchill's Empire: The World that Made Him and the World He Made* (2010)

Trilling, Daniel. *Bloody Nasty People: The Rise of Britain's Far Right* (2012)

Turner, Alwyn. *A Classless Society: Britain in the 1990s* (2014)

Vinen, Richard. *Thatcher's Britain: The Political and Social Upheavals of the 1980s* (2010)

Walker, Martin. *The National Front* (1977)

Ward, S. & MacKenzie, J. (eds). *British Culture and the End of Empire* (2001)

Webster, Nesta. *World Revolution: The Plot Against Civilisation* (1921)

Wellings, Ben. *English Nationalism and Euroscepticism: Losing the Peace* (2012)

Winder, Robert. *Bloody Foreigners: The Story of Immigration to Britain* (2005)

Wodak, R. et. al (eds). *Right-Wing Populism in Europe: Politics and Discourse* (2013)

INDEX

233